SPY AGENCIES, INTELLIGENCE OPERATIONS, AND THE PEOPLE BEHIND THEM

INTELLIGENCE and
COUNTERINTELLIGENCE

SPY AGENCIES, INTELLIGENCE OPERATIONS, AND THE PEOPLE BEHIND THEM

EDITED BY ROB CURLEY, SENIOR EDITOR,
SCIENCE AND TECHNOLOGY

Britannica®
Educational Publishing

IN ASSOCIATION WITH

ROSEN
EDUCATIONAL SERVICES

Published in 2013 by Britannica Educational Publishing
(a trademark of Encyclopædia Britannica, Inc.)
in association with Rosen Educational Services, LLC
29 East 21st Street, New York, NY 10010.

Distributed exclusively by Rosen Educational Services.
For a listing of additional Britannica Educational Publishing titles, call toll free (800) 237-9932.

First Edition

Britannica Educational Publishing
Rob Curley: Senior Editor, Science and Technology
J.E. Luebering: Senior Manager
Adam Augustyn: Assistant Manager
Marilyn L. Barton: Senior Coordinator, Production Control
Steven Bosco: Director, Editorial Technologies
Lisa S. Braucher: Senior Producer and Data Editor
Yvette Charboneau: Senior Copy Editor
Kathy Nakamura: Manager, Media Acquisition

Rosen Educational Services
Nicholas Croce: Editor
Nelson Sá: Art Director
Cindy Reiman: Photography Manager
Karen Huang: Photo Researcher
Brian Garvey: Designer, Cover Design
Introduction by Richard Barrington

Library of Congress Cataloging-in-Publication Data

Spy agencies, intelligence operations, and the people behind them/edited by Rob Curley.
    pages cm.—(Intelligence and counterintelligence)
"In association with Britannica Educational Publishing, Rosen Educational Services."
Includes bibliographical references and index.
ISBN 978-1-62275-035-1 (library binding)
1. Spies—Juvenile literature. 2. Spies—Vocational guidance—Juvenile literature.
3. Intelligence service—Juvenile literature. 4. Espionage—Juvenile literature. I. Curley, Rob.
JF1525.I6S73 2014
327.12—dc23

                                              2012046945
Manufactured in the United States of America

On the cover, pp. i, iii: The security control room for the 2012 Olympics in London. *AFP/ Getty Images*

CONTENTS

16

19

26

37

46

64

77

80

INTRODUCTION

The MI6 building in London, England. Dan Kitwood/Getty Images

For people who are supposed to live their lives in the shadows, some spies—real or fictional—have attained a very high profile in the popular consciousness over the years. James Bond, Mata Hari, and Jason Bourne are all household names, and there are plenty of others. This is not likely to change. Intelligence operations are a reality of the modern world, whether they are carried out for offensive or defensive purposes. This book will look at the some of the origins, personalities, and methods of modern espionage.

It's a surprisingly diverse subject, and one that goes well beyond the cat-and-mouse games depicted in movies. Whether your interest is in politics, computer technology, economics, or science—or even if you just love a good spy story—there should be something in this discussion of spy agencies and intelligence operations to interest you.

This book will move from the general to the specific, giving first some background on the nature of intelligence, and then discussing some of the history and personalities that have made their marks on the field—for better or worse. Finally, the book will bring the story right up to date, by discussing today's intelligence organizations.

In this context, the wide range of activities we know as "intelligence" can be sorted into the categories of strategic, tactical, and counterintelligence. Beyond the traditional role of intelligence being used to help countries keep tabs on adversarial states, in today's world it is often used to help guard against terrorism and other major crimes and to help protect technological infrastructure and trade secrets.

While intelligence activities may primarily involve information-gathering and analysis, at times intelligence agencies have played a more tangible role, including over-throwing governments and conducting assassinations. This helps account for the dramatic—and somewhat checkered—reputation that intelligence agencies have developed over the years. This book will discuss the various activities of intelligence agencies, including evaluating information available from public sources as well as conducting electronic surveillance, cyberespionage, and classic human spycraft.

Given the scope of their activities, intelligence agencies are major players on the world stage. If it were a corporation, for example, the Central Intelligence Agency (CIA) would be one of the world's more prominent companies, with around 20,000 employees in the United States. Naturally, though, the CIA prefers to keep a lower profile than the typical multibillion-dollar organization.

The roots of this giant of the intelligence community are surprisingly modest. While intelligence agencies were formed by most major powers in reaction to World War I, the United States was a latecomer to that secretive community. In fact, the United States entered World War II without a comprehensive intelligence organization. That was rectified in 1942 with the formation of the Office of Strategic Services, which evolved into the CIA in 1947.

Because it came into existence in the early days of the Cold War, much of the CIA's history involves the long-running intelligence chess match between the United States and the Soviet Union. This book will recap this history, including examples of covert operations that didn't become known until years after the fact. Along with some successes, the history of the CIA also includes failures such as the Bay of Pigs invasion, an international embarrassment that heightened Cold War tensions.

Naturally, its role in the Cold War often brought the CIA into direct conflict with the Soviet intelligence agency, the KGB. This book will also examine the often-sinister history of the KGB and its predecessors in the Soviet Union. A major distinction between the CIA and the Soviet intelligence agencies is that the CIA is forbidden from carrying out domestic operations, while a significant function of the Soviet intelligence apparatus was to help protect the country's leadership from internal threats. This resulted in the deaths of hundreds of thousands of Soviet citizens over the years and made the KGB a significant source of power within the Soviet Union.

Of course, not all the Soviet Union's intelligence efforts were directed within its own borders, and an early emphasis of the Cold War years was to gather information about U.S. atomic bomb technology. The Soviet Union had considered developing an atomic bomb throughout World War II, but by the time the U.S. exploded its first devices in 1945, it was clear that the Soviet Union's scientists lagged badly behind. The Soviets focused on catching up, and espionage was a major part of their effort.

This book will look at some of the major figures in the Soviet atomic espionage operation, people who were often operating within the Western scientific community. Some were caught—in the cases of Klaus Fuchs and Julius and Ethel Rosenberg, there were high-profile arrests soon after the fact. However, others were so successful that their roles didn't become known until after the collapse of the Soviet Union in 1991. In all, spies made a valuable contribution to the successful development of a Soviet atomic device by the end of the 1940s. In this way, spy agencies and intelligence operations not only participated heavily in the Cold War, but were instrumental in bringing about its greatest threat.

These atomic bomb spies were not the only agents who succeeded in working for the Soviet Union in Western nations. Also discussed in these pages is the infamous Cambridge spy ring in Great Britain. This spy ring may be the most prominent example of what was to become a staple of espionage lore—the double agent.

The Cambridge spy ring was so named because its members had been students at the University of Cambridge during the 1930s. They disagreed with the capitalist, democratic systems of Britain and the United States, and embraced communism instead. This book will show how members of this spy ring managed to work their way into highly sensitive positions in Britain and the United States, all the while acting as agents for the Soviet Union. One member of the Cambridge spy ring, Kim Philby, even held such key posts as head of counterespionage for MI6 (the British foreign intelligence agency) and chief liaison officer between British and U.S. intelligence.

The Cambridge spy ring was broken up in the 1950s. However, by the time most of its members fled to the Soviet Union, the damage had been done, in the form of key information passed to the communists and the likely deaths of several Western agents who were betrayed.

While the United States has seen nothing quite as cohesive as the Cambridge spy ring—at least, not as far as is known—it has also suffered its share of traitors who acted as enemy agents. Some of these stories will also be examined, including one of the most prominent espionage cases in U.S. history, the Alger Hiss affair.

Hiss had enjoyed a highly successful career in government, including serving as a law clerk for Supreme Court justice Oliver Wendell Holmes and as an adviser for Pres. Franklin Roosevelt. In 1948, he was accused of having been part of a pre-World War II, pro-communist spy ring. The case became highly controversial—the man who accused Hiss was an unreliable figure, and Hiss was found guilty not of espionage but rather of perjury in connection with testimony he gave to Congress. The guilt or innocence of Hiss was debated for decades, but perhaps the greatest significance of the case was in giving momentum to the House Committee on Un-American Activities and figures like Joseph McCarthy and Richard Nixon, who were quickly making the threat of communist espionage a major political issue in the United States.

In the decades following the Alger Hiss trial, a number of other spies working within the U.S. intelligence and military communities would be discovered—just as there were spies working for the West within the Soviet Union during this period. One noteworthy aspect of the Cold War espionage cases examined by this book is the range of motivations they represent. While the Cambridge spy ring and others seem to have been motivated by a pro-communist ideology, other spies over the years have been driven by other motivations, including love and money.

Like the Soviet Union itself, the Cold War is now part of history, but intelligence agencies remain a major element of national security in virtually all developed states. This book will bring intelligence into the 21st century by examining the state of these agencies today. First the book will look at how some of the most established intelligence communities—those in the United

States, Russia, and the United Kingdom—have evolved. Next, the book will look at how intelligence agencies are coping with—and impacting—two of the world's key hotspots, the Middle East and East Asia.

The intelligence structures of the United States, Russia, and the United Kingdom are instructive to study because many of the world's countries have adopted one of these three models for their own efforts. In the United States, the phrase "intelligence community" is especially relevant because the country employs several different agencies in espionage, analysis, and covert activities. While the CIA was created in part to centralize America's intelligence-gathering initiatives, a variety of other agencies still carry out intelligence and espionage activities, each with a different reporting structure and often with overlapping responsibilities. After the terrorist attacks of September 11, 2001, the Department of Homeland Security was created in an attempt to better coordinate the efforts of these diverse organisations.

Though the intelligence structure of the Soviet Union went through a series of reorganizations over the years, it was always more centralized than the U.S. model, taking on both international and domestic responsibilities. The domestic dimension meant that Soviet intelligence often played a critical role in the country's internal politics. While the Soviet Union no longer exists, intelligence agencies in modern Russia continue to follow some of the traditions of their Soviet predecessors.

Britain has the distinction of having one of the world's longest-running intelligence efforts. Like the U.S., it employs a multi-agency approach to distinguish domestic from international efforts, but there are differences. Information about the British intelligence community is kept more secret from the general public than in the United States, yet there is also more direct accountability to the government.

Each of these intelligence models must grapple with an ever-changing set of challenges, and different countries around the world put their own twist on intelligence practices. To wrap up its look at intelligence agencies today, this book will examine how key countries in two perennial trouble spots, the Middle East and East Asia, pursue their intelligence priorities.

In the Middle East, a volatile mix of religious tensions and oil revenues has kept the region on edge for decades. This book will focus on how two of today's major players in that drama, Israel and Iran, use their intelligence agencies to defend their interests and seek an upper hand over their enemies. Farther east, India and Pakistan face off over religious and territorial differences, and intelligence agencies play a recurring role there as well.

Another region that is prone to conflicts is East Asia. China's leaders grapple with trying to keep authoritarian control over their population, while transitioning to a more capitalist-based economy. Meanwhile, the country's split with Taiwan remains a sore point for both nations. Another uncomfortable rift is seen on the Korean peninsula. Here North Korea has a young, untested leader, crushing poverty, and a nuclear weapon—a most dangerous combination. Meanwhile, in South Korea many still long for reunification—but on the South's terms. All these conflicts keep intelligence activities buzzing in those countries, with additional participation from an outside world that looks on anxiously.

In books, movies, and television, spies are often glamorous characters doing adventurous things in exotic locations. In reality, though, espionage is serious work that raises serious questions. Do intelligence agencies help cope with tensions among countries, or do they merely heighten those tensions? Do intelligence agencies protect a country's citizens or intrude on their rights? These are some of the lingering questions surrounding spy agencies and intelligence operations. By providing some background on the history and methods of those organizations, this book can help you become better informed to answer those questions.

CHAPTER 1

THE NATURE OF INTELLIGENCE

I n the popular imagination, intelligence operations are almost exclusively activities that the intelligence community commonly calls "covert action," a term that refers to the collection, analysis, and distribution of information and to secret intervention in the political or economic affairs of other countries, which are usually enemies or opponents. But, in fact, most intelligence operations are conducted at a very basic level, where intelligence is simply the evaluation of information concerning the strength, activities, and probable courses of action of all foreign countries and nonstate actors. In either case, covert or open, dangerous or day-to-day, intelligence is an important part of the exercise of national power and a fundamental element in decision making regarding national security, defense, and foreign policy.

LEVELS OF INTELLIGENCE

Intelligence is conducted on three levels: strategic (sometimes called national), tactical, and counterintelligence. The broadest of these levels is strategic intelligence, which includes information about the capabilities and intentions of foreign countries. Tactical intelligence, sometimes called operational or combat intelligence, is information required by military field commanders. Because of the enormous destructive power of modern weaponry, the decision making of political leaders often must take into account information derived from tactical as well as strategic intelligence; major field commanders may often also need multiple levels of intelligence. Thus, the distinction between these two levels of intelligence may be vanishing.

Counterintelligence is aimed at protecting and maintaining the secrecy of a country's intelligence operations. Its purpose is to prevent spies or other agents of a foreign power from penetrating the country's government, armed services, or intelligence agencies. Counterintelligence also is concerned with protecting advanced technology, deterring terrorism, and combating international narcotics trafficking. Counterintelligence operations sometimes produce positive intelligence, including information about the intelligence-gathering tools and techniques of other countries and about the kinds of intelligence other countries may be seeking. Counterintelligence operations sometimes involve the manipulation of an adversary's intelligence services through the placement of "moles," or double agents, in sensitive areas. In authoritarian and totalitarian states, counterintelligence also encompasses the surveillance of key elites and the repression of dissent.

TYPES OF INTELLIGENCE

The types of intelligence a country may require are extremely varied. The country's armed services need military intelligence, its space and Earth-satellite programs need scientific intelligence, its foreign offices need political and biographical intelligence, and its premier or president needs a combination of these types and many others. Consequently, intelligence has become a vast

Central Intelligence Agency headquarters in Langley, Virginia.
Getty Images

industry. At the beginning of the 21st century it was estimated that the U.S. government spent some $30 billion annually on intelligence-related activities, employing perhaps 200,000 people in the United States and many thousands more U.S. citizens overseas in both clandestine and overt capacities. The intelligence operations of the Soviet Union were likely of even greater dimensions prior to the dissolution of the country in 1991. All other major countries maintain large intelligence bureaucracies.

Political intelligence is at once the most sought-after and the least reliable of the various types of intelligence. Because no one can predict with absolute certainty the effects of the political forces in a foreign country, analysts are reduced to making forecasts of alternatives based on what is known about political trends and patterns. Concrete data that are helpful in this regard include voting trends, details of party organization and leadership, and information derived from analyses of political documents. A chief source of political intelligence has long been the reports of diplomats, who normally gather data from "open," or legally accessible, sources in the country where they are stationed. Their work is supplemented by that of the professional intelligence apparatus.

Much military intelligence is gathered by military attachés, who have formal diplomatic status but are known to be mainly concerned with intelligence. Space satellites produce reliable information about the composition of military units and weapons and can track their movements; satellites are especially important for monitoring a country's production of strategic ballistic missiles and weapons of mass destruction (i.e., biological, chemical, and nuclear weapons). The most valuable kinds of military intelligence concern military organization and equipment, procedures and formations, and the number of units and total personnel.

The state of a country's economy is crucial to its military strength, its political development, and the conduct of its foreign policy. Consequently, intelligence organizations attach great importance to the collection of economic information, including data on trade, finance, natural resources, industrial capacity, and gross national product.

Because of continuous advances in technology, there has been a constant race between new methods of collecting intelligence and new techniques of protecting secret information. In order to guard against scientific or technological breakthroughs that may give other countries

Hexagon KH-9 Reconnaissance satellite. Paul J.Richards/AFP/Getty Images

a decisive advantage, intelligence organizations keep abreast of foreign advances in nuclear technology, in the electronic, chemical, and computer sciences, and in many other scientific fields.

In order to make accurate predictions of a foreign country's future behaviour, intelligence systems obviously require detailed information about the personal characteristics of the country's leaders. The need for biographical information has expanded with the proliferation of international organizations, whose officers must be briefed about their foreign counterparts. Intelligence agencies also compile data on foreign populations, topographies, climates, and a wide range of ecological factors.

SOURCES OF INTELLIGENCE

Despite the public image of intelligence operatives as cloak-and-dagger secret agents, the largest amount of intelligence work is an undramatic search of open sources, such as Internet traffic, radio broadcasts, and publications of all kinds. Much of this work, which also includes sifting reports from diplomats, businessmen, accredited military attachés, and other observers, is performed by university-trained research analysts in quiet offices.

Covert sources of intelligence fall into three major categories: imagery intelligence, which includes aerial and space reconnaissance; signals intelligence, which includes electronic eavesdropping and code breaking; and human intelligence, which involves the secret agent working at the classic spy trade. Broadly speaking, the relative value of these sources is reflected in the order in which they are listed above. A photograph, for example, constitutes hard (i.e., reliable) intelligence, whereas the report of a secret agent may be speculative and difficult to prove.

METHODS OF INTELLIGENCE GATHERING

Good intelligence management begins with the proper determination of what needs to be known. Unless precise requirements are set, data will be collected unsystem-atically and the decision maker ultimately left without pertinent information on which to act. Collected data must be evaluated and transformed into a usable form (and sometimes stored for future use). Evaluation is essen-tial, because many of the wide variety of sources are of doubtful reliability. A standardized system is used to rate the reliability of sources and the likely accuracy of the information they provide (e.g., information may be classified as confirmed, probably true, possibly true, or unlikely to be true).

Information obtained from open sources probably constitutes more than four-fifths of the input to most intelligence systems, though this proportion varies with the number of state secrets a country may have. Clandestine collection methods from covert sources provide the basis for much of the drama and romance attributed to intelligence work in fiction. Although the classic espionage agent will never be completely obsolete, some observers have suggested that the role largely has been taken over by machines, including orbiting reconnaissance satellites, long-range cameras, and a variety of sensing, detecting, and acoustical instruments. With this kind of technology, it is now possible to see in darkness, to hear from great distances, and to take detailed photographs from altitudes of hundreds of miles. Nevertheless, only spies can produce information about the attitudes and intentions of foreign leaders or international terrorists and other criminals. Indeed, a lack of adequate human intelligence was cited by some critics as a factor in the failure of U.S. intelligence and law-enforcement agencies to prevent the devastating terrorist attacks on New York City and Washington, D.C., on September 11, 2001.

Intelligence organizations often employ electronic scavengers (from ships, planes, listening posts in embassies and military installations, and orbiting satellites) to collect information about a country's radio communications and its naval equipment and operations. An individual submarine, for example, can be identified by the telltale and unique noises it makes (its "signature"). During the Cold War the United States collected sensitive signals

U-2 High-altitude reconnaissance aircraft. DOD/Getty Images

intelligence by tapping communications lines in Soviet territorial waters. It also used satellites and special planes for conducting missions close to the borders of potential adversaries. Similarly, the Soviet Union (and later Russia) collected signals intelligence from listening stations in diplomatic and consular missions and from large "fishing trawlers" that shadowed the U.S. fleet.

The use of computers to analyze data on complex phenomena such as industrial production, missile launches, and rates of economic growth has created vast amounts of information that threaten intelligence systems with inundation, making the filtering of useless information a key task. Since World War II great efforts have been made to

THE U-2 AFFAIR

On May 5, 1960, Soviet premier Nikita S. Khrushchev told the Supreme Soviet of the U.S.S.R. that an American U-2 reconnaissance plane had been shot down on May 1 over Sverdlovsk (now Yekaterinburg), referring to the flight as an "aggressive act" by the United States. On May 7 he revealed that the pilot of the plane, Francis Gary Powers, had parachuted to safety, was alive and well in Moscow, and had testified that he had taken off from Peshāwar, in Pakistan, with the mission of flying across the Soviet Union over the Aral Sea and via Sverdlovsk, Kirov, Arkhangelsk, and Murmansk to Bodö military airfield in Norway, collecting intelligence information en route. Powers admitted working for the U.S. Central Intelligence Agency.

On May 7 the United States stated that there had been no authorization for any such flight as Khrushchev had described, although a U-2 probably had flown over Soviet territory. The Soviet Union refused to accept that the U.S. government had had no knowledge of the flights and on May 13 sent protest notes to Turkey, Pakistan, and Norway, which in turn protested to the United States, seeking assurances that no U.S. aircraft would be allowed to use their territories for unauthorized purposes. On May 16 in Paris, Khrushchev declared that he could not take part in a long-planned summit conference with U.S. Pres. Dwight D. Eisenhower unless the U.S. government immediately stopped flights over Soviet territory, apologized for those already made, and punished the persons responsible. The response of Eisenhower, promising to suspend all such flights during the remainder of his presidency, did not satisfy the Soviet Union, and the conference was adjourned on May 17.

Francis Gary Powers was tried on August 17–19, 1960, and sentenced to 10 years' confinement. However, on February 10, 1962, in a ceremony on a bridge between West Berlin and East Germany, Powers and an American student who had been held without charge in East Germany since August 1961 were exchanged for Rudolf Abel, a Soviet intelligence officer who had been convicted in the United States in 1957 for conspiring to transmit military secrets to the Soviet Union. Powers returned to the United States and wrote of his view of the incident in *Operation Overflight* (1970). In 1977 he died in the crash of a helicopter that he flew as a reporter for a Los Angeles television station. Abel died of lung cancer in Moscow in 1971.

develop efficient means of cataloging, storing, and retrieving the gigantic volume of data being amassed. Although some observers believe that data collection, especially in the Internet age, has been overemphasized at the expense of analysis, computer technology and the application of artificial intelligence, which allow computer programs to organize mammoth amounts of raw material for analysts, promise to make the tidal wave of information manageable. For example, such techniques can be used at border crossings to quickly compare the image of a suspected terrorist with thousands of pictures of known criminals.

CYBERESPIONAGE

Cyberespionage and even cybersabotage are quintessential intelligence operations of the Internet age. Indeed, attempts to infiltrate or attack a country's information assets of national security or strategic economic importance have become so common that the U.S. Department of Defense has coined the term *advanced persistent threat* (APT) to refer specifically to cyberespionage efforts against American national security interests. Attacks by Chinese sources in 2009 against the search engine company Google and in 2011 against RSA, the security division of the information technology company EMC Corporation, brought the concept into discussions within the commercial information security community. Some authorities in that community advocated expanding the concept to include any sophisticated hacking campaign conducted against a large organization. However, the motive behind the threat goes beyond mere political or financial gain. An APT is not hacktivism—that is, penetrating a Web site or network to make a political statement—nor is it strictly cybercrime, where the perpetrators steal information for profit alone. Rather, the aim is to gain strategic or tactical advantage in the international arena.

Common targets of APTs include government agencies, defense contractors, and industries developing technologies of military or economic strategic importance, such as aerospace and computer companies. APTs use technology that minimizes their visibility to computer network and individual computer intrusion detection systems. Once an APT has entered its target, the attack can last for months or years; that is, it is a "persistent" threat. An example of this technology was the computer worm Stuxnet, which in 2010 was discovered to have infiltrated and corrupted devices that controlled nuclear centrifuges in Iran.

Specific items for data exfiltration (the stealing of knowledge) include e-mail archives, document stores, intellectual property containing trade secrets, and databases containing classified or proprietary information. Examples of targeted documents are product designs, supplier lists, research lab notes, and testing results.

Art Coviello, executive vice president, EMC corporation, speaks at an RSA conference. David Paul Morris/Getty Images

Methods of attack include "spear phishing" and the distribution of "zero-day malware." Spear phishing uses e-mails sent to selected employees within an organization. The e-mails appear to come from trusted or known sources. Either by clicking on links within the e-mail or by being persuaded by the e-mail's seeming legitimacy to let their guard down, these employees let hostile programs enter their computers. Zero-day malware is hostile computer software, such as viruses or Trojan horses, that is not yet detectable by antivirus programs. Networks of already compromised computers, known as "botnets," distribute these zero-day attacks. Neither of the methods is new, and they are not exclusive to APTs. Their use against national security assets, however, is indicative of an APT attack rather than conventional hacking.

APT attacks are by nature stealthy and may use software that is more sophisticated than common "off-the-shelf" hacking tools found on the Internet. Their footprint on a computer or network is relatively small, and APTs try to operate below the detection level of an intrusion-detection system. Discovering the APT, however, is still possible through close monitoring of traffic on a network. Identifying communications between the bot-net master (the control point) and the implanted malware reveals the compromise. This need for command-and-control activity remains the Achilles' heel of APTs.

CHAPTER TWO

TITANS OF THE COLD WAR: THE CIA AND THE KGB

During the Cold War, intelligence became one of the world's largest industries, employing hundreds of thousands of professionals. Every major country created enormous new intelligence bureaucracies, usually consisting of interlocking and often competitive secret agencies that vied for new assignments and sometimes withheld information from each other. The United States established the Central Intelligence Agency in 1947. Numerous allies of the United States had their own intelligence services, among them the United Kingdom's MI5 and MI6, France's SDECE (External Documentation and Counterespionage Service), and Israel's Mossad. But the great archrival of the West in the Cold War contest was the Soviet Union's KGB (Committee for State Security), created in 1954 to serve as the "sword and shield of the Communist Party."

At its peak the KGB was the largest secret-police and foreign-intelligence organization in the world. Researchers with access to Communist Party archives have put the number of KGB personnel at more than 480,000, including 200,000 soldiers in the Border Guards. Estimates of the number of informers in the Soviet Union are incomplete but usually range in the millions. Every Soviet leader depended on the KGB and its predecessors for information, surveillance of key elites, and control of the population. With the

KGB headquarters in Moscow. Pressphotos/Getty Images

Communist Party and the army, the KGB formed the triad of power that ruled the Soviet Union.

The KGB played a particularly important role in Soviet foreign policy. Foreign intelligence allowed the Soviet Union to maintain rough parity with the West in nuclear weapons and other weapons systems. Inside the country, however, the role of the KGB was baleful. Scholars disagree about the human cost of the KGB and its predecessors, but many estimate that they were responsible for the deaths of tens of millions of people.

The CIA, meanwhile, has been criticized for conducting covert actions that some consider immoral or illegal

under international law, for maintaining close ties to human rights abusers and other criminals, and for failing to safeguard its own operations. In the early days of the Cold War, the CIA and the U.S. military intelligence services smuggled former Nazi intelligence officers out of Europe, and the agency worked with several former Nazis to conduct intelligence operations in eastern Europe and the Soviet Union. In the 1980s and '90s, in an effort to infiltrate foreign terrorist organizations, the CIA recruited foreign officials, particularly in Latin America, who had participated in the murder of civilians.

After the terrorist attacks of September 2001, the CIA, along with the Federal Bureau of Investigation (FBI), was criticized for failing to penetrate terrorist groups that pose a threat to the United States and for failing to share information on such groups. In 2005 a presidential committee examining intelligence failures released a report that criticized the CIA for its inaccurate assessments of Ṣaddām Ḥussein's possession of weapons of mass destruction in the lead-up to the Iraq War.

Persistent criticism is almost inevitable, since the CIA faces far greater public scrutiny than the intelligence services of most other Western democracies. Its failures are trumpeted in the press, discussed on the floor of Congress, and frequently leaked to the media by ambitious policy makers. Apart from these problems, there exists a natural tension between the transparency and accountability essential to a democracy and the secrecy necessary for effective intelligence gathering.

THE CIA

Formally created in 1947, the CIA grew out of the World War II Office of Strategic Services (OSS). Previous U.S. intelligence and counterintelligence efforts had been conducted by the military and the FBI and suffered from duplication, competition, and lack of coordination, problems that continued, to some degree, into the 21st century.

THE EMERGENCE OF THE CIA

The United States was the last of the major powers to establish a civilian intelligence agency responsible for the collection of secret information for policy makers. Indeed, because of rivalries between army and navy intelligence offices, which did not want to jeopardize the "security" of their information, Pres. Franklin D. Roosevelt was not given sensitive information about Japan in the months before the Japanese attacked Pearl Harbor in December 1941. In June 1942 Roosevelt created the OSS to bring together the fragmented and uncoordinated strands of U.S. foreign intelligence gathering in a single organization. William J. ("Wild Bill") Donovan, who had spurred Roosevelt into creating an information agency, became head of the OSS upon its founding and was largely responsible for building the organization and for improving its ability to perform economic and political intelligence analysis for senior policy makers.

During World War II the OSS, with a staff of approximately 12,000, collected and analyzed information on areas of the world in which U.S. military forces were operating. It used agents inside Nazi-occupied Europe, including Berlin; carried out counterpropaganda and disinformation activities; produced analytical reports for policy makers; and staged special operations (e.g., sabotage and demolition) behind enemy lines to support guerrillas and resistance fighters. Before the Allied invasion of Normandy in June 1944, more than 500 OSS agents were working inside occupied France. Among reports commissioned from the OSS were assessments of German industry and war-making capability and a psychological profile of German dictator Adolf Hitler that concluded that he would likely commit suicide should Germany be defeated. Under Donovan's capable, if unorthodox, direction, the OSS was remarkably effective, despite the initial inexperience of most of its personnel. Its successes notwithstanding, the OSS was dismantled at the conclusion of the war.

In 1946 Pres. Harry S. Truman, recognizing the need for a coordinated postwar intelligence establishment, created by executive order a Central Intelligence Group and a National Intelligence Authority, both of which recruited key former members of the OSS. As in the days of the OSS, there were problems of distrust and rivalry between the new civilian agencies and the military intelligence services and the FBI. In 1947 Congress passed the National Security Act, which created the CIA. The CIA was given extensive power to conduct foreign intelligence operations, but it was forbidden by law from engaging in operations on U.S. soil.

THE CIA IN THE COLD WAR

The publication of post–Cold War memoirs by former agents and the release of declassified documents by the

National security meeting with Pres. Harry S. Truman (second from right). James Whitmore/Time & Life Pictures/Getty Images

United States and Russia have provided a fairly complete account of the CIA's activities, including both its successes and its failures. CIA data collection and analysis was important for arms-control negotiations with the Soviet Union throughout the Cold War and for determining U.S. strategy during the 1962 Cuban missile crisis, when Pres. John F. Kennedy relied on information gathered by the CIA through Soviet double agent Col. Oleg Penkovsky. During the 1970s and '80s, CIA agents in the Soviet military and the KGB provided information on the Soviet military-industrial complex. During the Cold War, CIA technical operations included the bugging of the Soviet military's major communications line in East Germany and the development of reconnaissance aircraft such as the U-2 and spy satellites capable of photographing targets as small as a rocket silo. Aerial reconnaissance—first by plane and then by satellite—provided early warning of the deployment of Soviet missiles in Cuba and the development of new missiles in the Soviet Union.

Among the Directorate of Operations' covert actions were the ouster of the premier of Iran, Mohammad Mosaddeq, and the restoration of the shah in 1953; the overthrow by military coup of the democratically elected leftist government of Guatemala in the following year; the organization of a "secret army" of Miao (Hmong) tribesmen to monitor the Ho Chi Minh Trail during the Vietnam War; the financial support of military officers plotting against the government of Chilean president Salvador Allende before the military coup there in 1973; and, in the 1980s, the arming and training of mujahideen guerrillas fighting the Soviet-backed government and the Soviet military in the Afghan War and the organizing, arming, and training of the Nicaraguan Contras fighting to overthrow that country's Sandinista government. (In the early 1960s the CIA briefly considered using illegal drugs to control foreign agents.)

Although many covert actions were highly successful, some were embarrassing failures, such as the abortive Bay of Pigs invasion of Cuba by CIA-sponsored Cuban émigrés in 1961. The CIA also was unsuccessful in its multiple attempts to assassinate Cuban leader Fidel Castro in the 1960s through agents recruited within the Cuban government as well as through contacts with the Mafia in the United States. Plots to kill or embarrass Castro included poisoning his cigars, lacing his cigars with a hallucinogen, providing him with

THE BAY OF PIGS INVASION

On April 17, 1961, some 1,500 Cuban exiles opposed to the rule of revolutionary Fidel Castro landed at the Bahía de Cochinos (Bay of Pigs) on the southwestern coast of Cuba. The invasion, financed and directed by the U.S. government, was a fiasco. No coordination had been achieved with dissidents inside Cuba, and the failure to provide U.S. air cover doomed the invasion. Castro's army killed or captured most of the 1,500-man force in two days.

Within six months of Castro's overthrow of Fulgencio Batista's dictatorship in January 1959, relations between Castro's government and the United States began to deteriorate. The new Cuban government confiscated private property (much of it owned by North American interests), sent agents to initiate revolutions in several Latin-American countries, and established diplomatic and economic ties with leading socialist powers. Castro himself often and vociferously accused the United States of trying to undermine his government. Several U.S. congressmen and senators, from early 1960, denounced Castro; and by June the Congress had passed legislation enabling Pres. Dwight D. Eisenhower to take retaliatory steps: the United States cut off sugar purchases from Cuba and soon thereafter placed an embargo on all exports to Cuba except food and medicine. In January 1961, Eisenhower, in one of the final acts of his administration, broke diplomatic ties with Cuba.

An invasion of Cuba had been planned by the CIA since May 1960. The wisdom of proceeding with the invasion had been debated within the newly inaugurated administration of Pres. John F. Kennedy before it was finally approved and carried out.

On April 15, 1961, three U.S.-made airplanes piloted by Cubans bombed Cuban air bases. Two days later the Cubans trained by the United States and using U.S. equipment landed at several sites. The principal landing took place at the Bay of Pigs on the south-central coast. The invasion force was unequal to the strength of Castro's troops, and by April 19 its last stronghold had been captured, along with more than 1,100 men. In the aftermath of the invasion, critics charged the CIA with supplying faulty information to the new president and also noted that, in spite of Kennedy's orders, supporters of Batista were included in the invasion force, whereas members of the noncommunist People's Revolutionary Movement, considered the most capable anti-Castro group, were excluded.

The captured members of the invasion force were imprisoned. From May 1961 the Kennedy administration unofficially backed attempts to ransom the prisoners, but the efforts of the Tractors for Freedom Committee, headed by Eleanor Roosevelt, failed to raise the $28 million needed for heavy-construction equipment demanded by Castro as reparations. The conditions for the ransom changed several times during the next several months; after painstaking negotiations by James B. Donovan, Castro finally agreed to release the prisoners in exchange for $53 million worth of food and medicine. Between December 1962 and July 1965 the survivors were returned to the United States.

exploding cigars, poisoning his wet suit (Castro was an underwater enthusiast), and administering drugs that would cause his beard and eyebrows to fall out.

After the collapse of the Soviet Union in 1991, the CIA changed both its institutional structure and its mission. Whereas more than half its resources before 1990 had been devoted to activities aimed at the Soviet Union, in the post-Cold War era it increasingly targeted nonstate actors such as terrorists and international criminal organizations. It also made significant efforts to collect and analyze information about the proliferation of nuclear weapons. Spy satellites that had been used exclusively for military purposes were sometimes used for other tasks, such as collecting evidence of ecological disasters and human rights abuses.

THE KGB

The Komitet Gosudarstvennoy Bezopasnosti, in English the Committee for State Security but known to history as the KGB, was the foreign intelligence and domestic security agency of the Soviet Union. During the Soviet era the KGB's responsibilities also included the protection of the country's political leadership, the supervision of border troops, and the general surveillance of the population.

EARLY SOVIET SECURITY SERVICES

Established in 1954, the KGB was the most durable of a series of security agencies starting with the first days of the Bolshevik government in 1917. In 1941, during World War II, responsibility for state security was transferred from the prewar NKVD (People's Commissariat of Internal Affairs) to the NKGB (People's Commissariat for State Security). Both agencies became ministries — the Ministry of Internal Affairs (MVD) and the Ministry of State Security (MGB) — in 1946. Lavrenty Beria, the head of the NKVD from 1938, supervised the two ministries while serving as head of the MVD. Beria also was responsible for the Soviet Union's nascent nuclear weapons program and oversaw intelligence operations directed at the U.S. and British atomic bomb projects.

The MGB, directed by V.S. Abakumov under Beria's supervision, played a major role in the Soviet Union's war effort in World War II and in the subsequent consolidation of its power in eastern Europe. During the war, the MGB conducted espionage and counter-espionage operations, administered prisoner-of-war camps, and ensured the loyalty of the officer corps. After the war, the MGB helped to crush all opposition, whether real or suspected, in eastern Europe and the Soviet Union; between 1945 and 1953 more than 750,000 Soviet citizens were arrested and punished for political crimes. Information uncovered in the 1990s indicated that by 1953 some 2,750,000 Soviet citizens were in jail or in forced-labour camps, and approximately the same number were in internal exile.

Soviet foreign intelligence in the last decade of Joseph Stalin's life was remarkable in both its scope and success. During World War II the MGB conducted operations in Nazi-occupied Europe. One of its networks, the "Red Orchestra," comprised several hundred agents and informers, including agents in the German ministries of foreign affairs, labour, propaganda, and economics. Declassified Russian and American documents indicate that the Soviet Union had placed at least five agents in the U.S. nuclear weapons program and possibly as many as 300 agents in the U.S. government by 1945. The British diplomatic and security establishments also had been infiltrated by important agents, including Kim Philby, a senior British intelligence officer. Evidence suggests that Soviet agents in Britain passed 15,000 to 20,000 documents to Moscow between 1941 and 1945. British and American agents of Soviet intelligence were for the most part ideological supporters of the regime, and many were members of communist parties.

Immediately following Stalin's death in March 1953, the MGB was merged back into the Ministry of Internal

Affairs (MVD), still under Beria. Before the end of summer, the post-Stalinist leadership under Nikita Khrushchev turned against the power-hungry Beria, and he was deposed and executed. A series of trials and executions continuing into 1956 eliminated a number of his senior associates. In the meantime, millions of political prisoners were released from the MVD's vast system of forced labour camps and from internal exile. The MVD was gradually dismantled and finally abolished in 1960.

CREATION AND ROLE OF THE KGB

The KGB was designed to be carefully controlled by senior Communist Party officials. It was divided into approximately 20 directorates, the most important of which were those responsible for foreign intelligence, domestic counterintelligence, technical intelligence, protection of the political leadership, and the security of the country's frontiers. In the late 1960s an additional directorate was created to conduct surveillance on suspected dissidents in the churches and among the intelligentsia. For the next 20 years the KGB became increasingly zealous in its pursuit of enemies, harassing, arresting, and sometimes exiling human rights advocates, Christian and Jewish activists, and intellectuals judged to be disloyal to the regime.

On foreign soil, the KGB's many agents sometimes posed as businessmen and journalists, though many used the more conventional diplomatic cover. Its successes included the infiltration of every major Western intelligence operation and the placement of agents of influence in almost every major capital. The KGB also was able to procure scientific and technical information

Boris Yeltsin, 1991. Vario Press— Camera Press/Globe Photos

for the Soviet military, and it repeatedly obtained advanced technology necessary for the development of Soviet submarines, airplanes, and rockets. Along with the GRU (Chief Intelligence Directorate of the General Staff), which was responsible for purely military operations, the KGB enjoyed tremendous access to the secrets of both its adversaries and its allies.

By the end of the 1960s, the KGB had become firmly established as the Communist Party's security watchdog. Its value as an instrument of political control was reflected in the appointment of its head, Yury Andropov, to the Politburo (1973) and his succession to the head of the party and the country in 1982. Under Andropov, the KGB recruited the "best and the brightest" members from the party establishment. Although it was aware of the extent of corruption in the decaying Soviet Union and did investigate and arrest some minor figures, it continued to be a servant of the party and was thus powerless to halt the country's decline.

The KGB did not fare as well under the reformist Soviet leader Mikhail Gorbachev (1985–91). Although Gorbachev respected the KGB's prowess in foreign intelligence, his reform agenda undercut its authority as well as that of the Communist Party. In the summer of 1991, several senior KGB officers, including KGB chairman Vladimir Kryuchkov, played key roles in an abortive coup designed to return the Soviet system to ideological and bureaucratic purity. Afterward the KGB was systematically stripped of its extensive military units and many of its domestic security functions.

With the dissolution of the Soviet Union in 1991, the KGB came under the control of Russia. The government of Russian President Boris Yeltsin supervised the division of the KGB into several major services responsible for internal security and foreign intelligence.

CHAPTER THREE

SOVIET ATOMIC BOMB SPIES

The role of espionage in the making of the Soviet atomic bomb was first acknowledged in the early 1950s, with the arrests in Britain of the German-born Klaus Fuchs and in the United States of the American couple Julius and Ethel Rosenberg. Information made available from Russian sources following the breakup of the Soviet Union in 1991, however, demonstrated that espionage was more extensive than previously known and was more important to the Soviets' success. Throughout the war and afterward, spymaster Lavrenty Beria's agents amassed significant amounts of technical data that saved nuclear physicist Igor Kurchatov and his team, charged with developing the Soviet bomb, valuable time and scarce resources. The first Soviet test occurred on August 29, 1949, using a plutonium device that was a direct copy of the U.S. bomb dropped on Nagasaki, Japan, in 1945. It was based on plans supplied by Fuchs and by Theodore Hall, the latter a second key spy at Los Alamos whose activities were revealed only after the dissolution of the Soviet Union.

KLAUS FUCHS

Emil Klaus Julius Fuchs was born on December 29, 1911, in Rüsselsheim, Germany. He studied physics and mathematics at the Universities of Leipzig and Kiel and joined the German Communist Party in 1930. Forced to flee Germany after the Nazis came to power in 1933, he ended up in Great Britain, where he studied at the University of Edinburgh and received a doctorate there. He was briefly interned as a German at the start of World War II but was soon released in order to do research on the atomic bomb at the University of Birmingham. In 1942 he became a British citizen. When Fuchs realized the importance of the research he was engaged upon, he began passing scientific secrets on to the Soviet Union.

Klaus Emil Julius Fuchs leaving prison after serving a sentence for disclosing nuclear secrets to Russia. Evening Standard/Hulton Archive/Getty Images

In 1943 he was sent to the United States to work on the atomic bomb project at Los Alamos, where he acquired a thorough knowledge of the theory and design of the bomb and passed his knowledge on to the Soviets. His espionage is credited with saving the Soviets at least one year's work in their own program to develop the atomic bomb.

After the war he returned to England, where he became head of the physics department of the British nuclear research centre at Harwell. His espionage activities were finally detected, and he was arrested in 1950, upon which he admitted passing information to the Soviet Union since 1943. He was sentenced to 14 years in prison. After his release in 1959 for good behaviour, he went to East Germany, where he was granted citizenship and was appointed deputy director of the Central Institute for Nuclear Research, Rossendorf (near Dresden). He remained a committed communist and received many honours from the East German Communist Party and the scientific establishment there. He died on January 28, 1988, in East Germany.

RUTH WERNER

Ursula Ruth Kuczynski was born on May 15, 1907, in Berlin. She was a committed communist who operated as a spy for the Soviet Union in China, Nazi Germany, Switzerland, and England beginning in about 1930. Using the code name Sonya, she gathered and transmitted classified intelligence to Moscow, including technical information supplied by Klaus Fuchs about the Manhattan Project's research into the atomic bomb. After World War II she settled in East Germany, where she took the pen name Ruth Werner and became

ROBERT LAMPHERE: COUNTERINTELLIGENCE AGENT

Robert Joseph Lamphere was born on February 14, 1918, in Wardner, Idaho. He joined the FBI in 1941 after graduating from the National Law School, Washington, D.C. In 1947 Lamphere began work on the bureau's Soviet espionage squad as a counterintelligence specialist. He used deciphered Soviet cables to build cases against numerous spies—most notably Klaus Fuchs, who was convicted in 1950 for having given vital atomic-research secrets to the Soviet Union, and Julius and Ethel Rosenberg, who were found guilty of having passed military secrets to the Soviets and were executed in 1953. After leaving the FBI in 1955, Lamphere worked for the Veterans Administration and later as an insurance company executive. His memoir, *The FBI-KGB War: A Special Agent's Story*, appeared in 1986. He died on January 7, 2002, in Tucson, Arizona.

a celebrated writer of short stories, novels, and an autobiography, *Sonja's Rapport* (1977; *Sonya's Report*, 1991). She died on July 7, 2000, in Berlin.

ALAN NUNN MAY

Alan Nunn May was born on May 2, 1911, in Birmingham, England. After receiving his early education in Birmingham, he earned a degree in physics from the University of Cambridge. In 1942 Nunn May began working with the British branch of the Manhattan Project to study the feasibility of German plans to develop an atomic

Alan Nunn. ©TopFoto/The Image Works

bomb, and the following year the members of the project were transferred to Montreal, where he was recruited by Soviet military intelligence. Secrets he supplied to his handler included samples of enriched uranium and details of the bomb that was dropped on Hiroshima, Japan. In 1945, about the time Nunn May returned to Britain, a Soviet agent based in Ottawa defected with documents that implicated Nunn May, and in 1946 he was arrested, convicted, and sentenced to 10 years' hard labour, of which he served 6 years. He died on January 12, 2003, in Cambridge.

BRUNO PONTECORVO

Bruno Pontecorvo was born on August 22, 1913, in Marina di Pisa, Italy, one of eight children born to a Jewish textile merchant. He received his doctorate from the University of Rome, where in the early 1930s he worked with Enrico Fermi. After Mussolini's government passed a series of race laws, Pontecorvo fled to Paris to continue his research. When Paris was invaded by the Germans in 1940, he made his way to the United States. In 1943 Pontecorvo joined the Anglo-Canadian nuclear research team at Chalk River in Canada. He experimented with cosmic rays and with tritium, an element important for the making of the hydrogen bomb. In 1948 he became a British citizen, and the following year he joined the Atomic Energy Authority research station at Harwell, Berkshire, England, where classified research was being conducted.

While on vacation in Italy in 1950, Pontecorvo, his wife, and three children abruptly left for Stockholm. They then went to Helsinki, Finland, and were not heard from until 1955, when Pontecorvo appeared at a press conference in Moscow to promote the peaceful use of nuclear power. His disappearance had followed revelations that some highly placed scientists (including Klaus Fuchs, one of Pontecorvo's colleagues at Harwell) had given secrets to the Soviet Union and raised fears about how seriously these scientists had endangered the West. Pontecorvo denied ever having worked on nuclear weapons research. While in the Soviet Union, he worked at the Joint Institute for Nuclear Research outside Moscow. He received numerous awards from the state, including the Lenin Prize (1963) and the Order of Lenin (1983). He died on September 25, 1993, in Dubna, Russia.

THEODORE HALL

Theodore Alvin Hall was born on October 20, 1925, in New York City. An extremely precocious youngster, he graduated from high school in Brooklyn, New York, at the age of 14 and passed the entrance examination to Columbia University in Manhattan. Eventually he studied at Harvard University, Cambridge, Massachusetts, graduating with a degree in physics at the age of 18. Following the recommendation of a college professor, in January 1944 he reported to Los Alamos, New Mexico, where he became the youngest person to work on the Manhattan Project.

Hall worked on a team that designed an implosion device that would initiate the explosion of the plutonium core of an atomic bomb. Their design was tested successfully at Trinity, the first explosion of an atomic device, at Alamogordo, New Mexico, on July 16, 1945. By that time Hall had contacted Saville Sax, a boyhood friend and college roommate who had connections in left-wing politics. The two arranged a meeting with an agent of Soviet intelligence in New York City, where

Hall handed over details on the organization of work at Los Alamos. In subsequent deliveries, mediated by Sax or a Soviet agent, Hall handed over technical details that contributed directly to the Soviet Union's first atomic bomb, which was tested in 1949.

After the war Hall left Los Alamos and moved to Chicago, where he earned a doctorate in physics at the University of Chicago and worked in a biophysics laboratory. He maintained intermittent contact with Soviet agents for several more years, though it is not known what other information, if any, he passed on to them. In 1951 he and Sax were interrogated by the FBI, which had received decryptions of communiqués transmitted by the Soviets during the war that incriminated the two. No charges were ever brought against them, however, possibly because the communiqués were not sufficient to support prosecution or possibly because the authorities did not wish to reveal the extent of their decryption efforts.

After his interrogation and the arrest that same year of Julius and Ethel Rosenberg, Hall severed connections with left-wing political groups, and he and his family moved to New York City. There Hall worked at the Sloan-Kettering Institute for Cancer Research until 1962, when he accepted an invitation to conduct biological research at the Cavendish Laboratory of the University of Cambridge, England. He worked on applications of electron microscopy until he retired in 1984. In the 1990s the U.S. government declassified portions of its postwar decryption program, and Hall's wartime espionage became known. Hall never described his actions in detail, insisting for the rest of his life that he had acted out of youthful idealism, to prevent the United States from holding a dangerous monopoly over nuclear weapons. He died on November 1, 1999, in Cambridge.

JULIUS AND ETHEL ROSENBERG

Both Julius Rosenberg and Ethel Greenglass were born in New York City, Julius on September 28, 1915, and Ethel on May 12, 1918. Ethel worked as a clerk for some years after her graduation from high school in 1931. When she married Julius in 1939, the year he earned a degree in electrical engineering, the two were already active members of the Communist Party. In the following year Julius obtained a job as a civilian engineer with the U.S. Army Signal Corps, and he and Ethel began working together to disclose U.S. military secrets to the Soviet Union. Later, Ethel's brother, Sgt. David Greenglass, who was assigned as a machinist to the Manhattan Project to build the atomic bomb, provided the Rosenbergs with data on nuclear weapons. The Rosenbergs turned over this information to Harry Gold, a Swiss-born courier for the espionage ring, who then passed it to Anatoly A. Yakovlev, the Soviet Union's vice-consul in New York City.

Julius Rosenberg was discharged by the army in 1945 for having lied about his membership in the Communist Party. Gold was arrested on May 23, 1950, in connection with the case of the British spy Klaus Fuchs, who had been arrested for giving U.S. and British nuclear secrets to the Soviet Union. The arrests of Greenglass and Julius Rosenberg followed quickly in June and July, and Ethel was arrested in August. Another conspirator, Morton Sobell, a college classmate of Julius Rosenberg, fled to Mexico but was extradited.

The Rosenbergs were charged with espionage and brought to trial on March 6, 1951; Greenglass was the chief witness for the prosecution. On March 29 they were found guilty, and on April 5 the couple was sentenced to death. (Sobell and Gold received 30-year prison terms, and Greenglass, who was tried separately, was sentenced

A demonstration in Paris in 1953 calling for the pardon of Julius and Ethel Rosenberg. Keystone/Hulton Archive/Getty Images

to 15 years in prison.) For two years the Rosenberg case was appealed through the courts and before world opinion. The constitutionality and applicability of the Espionage Act of 1917, under which the Rosenbergs were tried, as well as the impartiality of the trial judge, Irving R. Kaufman— who in pronouncing sentence had accused them of a crime "worse than murder"—were key issues during the appeals process. Seven different appeals reached the Supreme Court of the United States and were denied, and pleas for executive clemency were dismissed by Pres. Harry Truman in 1952 and Pres. Dwight Eisenhower in 1953. A worldwide campaign for mercy failed, and the Rosenbergs were executed on June 19, 1953, in the electric chair at Sing Sing Prison in Ossining, New York. They were the first American civilians to be executed for espionage and the first to suffer that penalty during peacetime. Ethel became the first woman executed by the U.S. government since Mary Surratt was hanged in 1865 for her alleged role in the assassination of Abraham Lincoln.

In the years after the Rosenbergs' executions, there was significant debate about their guilt. The two were frequently regarded as victims of cynical and vindictive officials of the FBI. Highly sympathetic portraits of the Rosenbergs were offered in major novels, including E.L. Doctorow's *The Book of Daniel* (1971) and Robert Coover's *The Public Burning* (1977). (The former was released as the motion picture *Daniel* in 1983.) The controversy over their guilt was largely resolved in the early 1990s after the fall of communism in the Soviet Union and the release of Soviet intelligence information that confirmed the Rosenbergs' involvement in espionage.

CHAPTER FOUR

THE CAMBRIDGE SPY RING

At the University of Cambridge, England, in the 1930s, a group of upper-class students—including Guy Burgess, Donald Maclean, Kim Philby, and Anthony Blunt—shared a disdain for capitalist democracy and despaired of its ever having the strength to stop the rise of fascism. These men were recruited by Soviet intelligence operatives, by British intellectuals sympathetic to communism, and even by one another to become secret agents, and their careers as spies had astonishing success during and after World War II. Philby became head of counterespionage for MI6, the British foreign intelligence service; Burgess and Maclean worked for MI6 in various capacities, including postings in Washington, D.C.; and Blunt not only worked for MI5, the domestic security agency, but also became a respected art historian and a member of the queen's household. From these positions they were able to pass great amounts of invaluable information to the Soviet Union.

The ring unraveled in 1951, when Burgess and Maclean learned they were under investigation and fled under mysterious circumstances to Moscow. It was immediately assumed that a "third man" had warned the pair that they were in danger; one of those suspected was Philby, and these suspicions were confirmed 12 years later when he too defected. It was disclosed in 1979 that the aging Blunt was the "fourth man" who had contacted Soviet agents to arrange for Burgess and Maclean's escape. In the 1990s an elderly literary scholar named John Cairncross was named as a "fifth man," who was not on intimate terms with the other four but knew them and, like them, was "handled" by the same Soviet agent in charge of maintaining the Cambridge spy ring.

KIM PHILBY

Harold Adrian Russell Philby was born on January 1, 1912, in Ambala, India. While a student at the University of Cambridge, Philby became a Communist and in 1933 a Soviet agent. He worked as a journalist until 1940, when Guy Burgess, a British secret agent who was himself a Soviet double agent, recruited Philby into the MI6 section of the British intelligence service. By the end of World War II, Philby had become head of counterespionage operations for MI6, in which post he was responsible for combating Soviet subversion in western Europe. In 1949 he was sent to Washington to serve as chief MI6 officer there and as the top liaison officer between the British and U.S. intelligence services. While holding this highly sensitive post, he revealed to the U.S.S.R. an Allied plan to send armed anti-Communist bands into Albania in 1950, thereby assuring their defeat; warned two Soviet double agents in the British diplomatic service, Burgess and Donald Maclean, that they were under suspicion (the two men consequently escaped to the Soviet Union in 1951); and transmitted detailed information about MI6 and the Central Intelligence Agency to the Soviets.

After Burgess's and Maclean's defection, suspicion fell on Philby, and he was relieved of his intelligence duties

Harold Adrian Russell Philby in Moscow in 1968. Paul Popper/Popperfoto/Getty Images

in 1951 and dismissed from MI6 in 1955. Thereafter he worked as a journalist in Beirut until fleeing to the Soviet Union in 1963. There he settled in Moscow and eventually reached the rank of colonel in the KGB, the Soviet intelligence service. Philby published a book, *My Silent War* (1968), detailing his exploits.

Philby, the most successful Soviet double agent of the Cold War period, seems to have been a lifelong and committed Communist whose primary devotion lay toward the Soviet Union rather than toward his native country. He was apparently responsible for the deaths of many Western agents whose activities he betrayed to

the Soviets during the 1940s and early '50s. He died on
May 11, 1988, in Moscow.

GUY BURGESS

Guy Francis de Moncy Burgess was born in 1911 in Devonport,
Devon, England. The son of a Royal Navy officer, he was edu-
cated at the elite Eton College and Dartmouth Naval College
before entering Trinity College, Cambridge. He graduated in
1933 with a degree in history but remained for two years on
a postgraduate teaching fellowship. At Cambridge, Burgess
quickly acquired a reputation for cleverness, drunkenness,
and promiscuous homosexual behaviour. He circulated
among a number of left-leaning students and acquaintances,
including Blunt, Philby, and Maclean, but it has never been
established with certainty who recruited him into working
for Soviet intelligence. In any case, Burgess began supplying
information from his posts as a BBC correspondent from
1936 to 1938, a member of the MI6 intelligence agency from
1938 to 1941, and a member of the British Foreign Office
from 1944.

In 1951 Burgess was recalled from his post as second secretary of the British embassy in Washington, D.C. He was
about to be dismissed from the Foreign Service when he
learned in May of that year that a counterintelligence investigation by British and U.S. agencies was closing in on his
Cambridge colleague Maclean. To avoid prosecution, both
men fled England; their whereabouts remained unknown
until 1956, when they held a press conference to announce
that they were living as communists in Moscow. In 1963 they
were joined by Philby, another Cambridge and Foreign Office
colleague, who, it was revealed, had given them the warning
in 1951. On August 30 of that same year, Burgess, his health
broken by alcoholism, died of a heart attack in Moscow.

DONALD MACLEAN

Donald Maclean was born on May 25, 1913, in London. Recruited as an agent by Soviet intelligence operatives while circulating among left-wing groups at the University of Cambridge (where he met Guy Burgess), he began supplying information as a member of the British Foreign Office from 1934.

As first secretary and then head of chancery at the British embassy in Washington, D.C., Maclean gained the post of secretary of the Combined Policy Committee on Atomic Development and was privy to highly classified information. He also supplied the Soviet Union with secret

Donald Maclean. Keystone/Hulton Archive/Getty Images

material relating to the formation of the North Atlantic Treaty Organization. As head of the American department at the Foreign Office in 1950, he helped formulate Anglo-American policy for the Korean War.

In May 1951 Maclean received a warning that a counter-intelligence investigation by British and U.S. agencies was targeting him. Along with Burgess, who was also acting as a spy, he fled England and mysteriously vanished. No trace of the two men appeared until 1956, when they surfaced in Moscow and announced their long-standing allegiance

THE PROFUMO AFFAIR

At a party at the country estate of Lord Astor on July 8, 1961, British Secretary of State for War John Profumo, then a rising 46-year-old Conservative Party politician, was introduced to 19-year-old London dancer Christine Keeler by Stephen Ward, an osteopath with contacts in both the aristocracy and the underworld. Also present at this gathering was a Russian military attaché, Yevgeny Ivanov, who was Keeler's lover. Through Ward's influence Profumo began an affair with Keeler, and rumours of their involvement soon began to spread. In March 1963 Profumo lied about the affair to Parliament, stating that there was "no impropriety whatsoever" in his relationship with Keeler. Evidence to the contrary quickly became too great to hide, however, and, 10 weeks later Profumo resigned, admitting "with deep remorse" that he had deceived the House of Commons.

The scandal, involving sex, a Russian spy, and the secretary of state for war, captured the attention of the British public and discredited the government. Conservative Prime Minister Harold Macmillan continued in office until October, but the scandal was pivotal in his eventual downfall, and within a year the opposition Labour Party defeated the Conservatives in a national election.

Despite charges of attempted espionage, neither the FBI nor British intelligence was able to confirm or deny that Ivanov had attempted to entrap Profumo or to use Keeler as an access agent. Ivanov left Britain before the scandal became public, attending the Academy of the General Staff and later serving in important intelligence positions until his retirement in 1981.

Following her trial, in which she was convicted of perjury and conspiracy, Keeler sank into obscurity, though in 2001 she wrote an autobiography, which many considered an essentially worthless account of the affair. Ward committed suicide on the last day of his trial for pimping. Profumo rebuilt his life by working for the next four decades, initially washing dishes, at Toynbee Hall (in London's East End), which offered help and comfort for the city's poor. He never spoke publicly about the scandal that bore his name, and in later life he was widely praised for having risen from disgrace to redemption. Because of his charity work, Profumo was named Commander of the British Empire (C.B.E.) in 1975. He died on March 9, 2006, in London.

to communism. In 1963 they were joined by Kim Philby, another Cambridge and Foreign Office colleague, who, it was revealed, had given them the warning in 1951. Not until 1979 was it made public that the inferred "fourth man" in the spy ring was Anthony Blunt, a respected art historian and member of the queen's household. It had been Blunt, also a Cambridge colleague, who had contacted Soviet agents to arrange for Maclean's and Burgess's escape from England. Maclean died in Moscow on March 11, 1983.

ANTHONY BLUNT

Anthony Frederick Blunt was born on September 26, 1907, in Bournemouth, Hampshire, England. While a fellow of Trinity College, Cambridge, in the 1930s Blunt became a member of a circle of disaffected young men that included Guy Burgess, and he was soon involved in espionage on behalf of the Soviet Union. His public career was brilliant. From 1937 he published scores of scholarly papers and books by which he largely established art history in Great Britain. He was an authority on 17th-century painting, particularly that of Nicolas Poussin. During World War II he served in MI5, a military intelligence organization, and was able to supply secret information to the Soviets

Anthony Frederick Blunt. Lee/Hulton Archive/Getty Images

and, more importantly, to give warning to fellow agents of counterintelligence operations that might endanger them.

In 1945 Blunt was appointed surveyor of the king's (later the queen's) pictures, and in 1947 he became director of the Courtauld Institute, one of the world's leading centres of training and research in art history. His major publications in subsequent years included *Art and Architecture in France 1500–1700* (1953) and *Nicolas Poussin* (1966–67). Although his active intelligence work had apparently ceased in 1945, he maintained contacts with Soviet agents and in 1951 was able to arrange for the escape of Burgess and Donald Maclean from Britain. In 1964, after the defection of Kim Philby, he was confronted by British authorities and secretly confessed his Soviet connections. Not until 1979, seven years after he retired from his posts, was his past made public. In the outcry that surrounded his being revealed as the long-sought "fourth man" in the spy ring, he was stripped of the knighthood that had been awarded him in 1956.

Blunt died in London on March 26, 1983. In 2009 the British Library released to the public his memoir. Although he wrote that being a Soviet spy was "the biggest mistake" of his life, Blunt failed to provide much information about his espionage work.

JOHN CAIRNCROSS

John Cairncross was born on July 25, 1913, in Lesmahagow, Scotland. The son of an ironmonger, he graduated from Glasgow University in 1933 with a degree in German and French. He studied modern languages at the Sorbonne in Paris and then at Trinity College, University of Cambridge. At Cambridge he frequented left-wing circles and met other members of the future spy ring, but he did not fit in with the polished young men and pursued his future careers apart from them.

In 1936 Cairncross passed the civil service entrance examinations with outstanding marks and entered the Foreign Office. Shortly after, he was introduced by James Klugmann, a communist from Cambridge, to a Soviet agent who invited him to aid the antifascist movement. Cairncross was transferred in 1938 to the Treasury and in 1940, after the start of World War II, to the Cabinet Office, where he became the private secretary of Sir Maurice Hankey, the chancellor of the Duchy of Lancaster. In this latter capacity Cairncross may have passed to the Soviets a copy of the MAUD report, which evaluated Britain's prospects for building an atomic bomb.

In 1942 he was assigned as a German translator to Bletchley Park, a government research centre north of London where encrypted German military communications were decoded and disseminated to intelligence services. Cairncross smuggled many decrypted German communiqués to the Soviets, including vital messages on army movements on the Eastern Front that helped the Red Army to prepare for the Germans' huge tank offensive at the Battle of Kursk (July–August 1943).

In 1944 Cairncross returned to the Treasury. After the war he may have passed plans for the new North Atlantic Treaty Organization alliance to the Soviets. In 1951, after Donald Maclean and Guy Burgess had fled England to escape investigation, notes written by Cairncross were found in Burgess's home, and Cairncross was interrogated by MI5, the British domestic security agency. Cairncross denied having spied for the Soviets, but he agreed to resign from the Civil Service. He began a new career as a literary scholar, teaching in the United States at Northwestern University in Illinois and at Case Western Reserve University in Ohio. Over the following decades he published a number of translations and studies of the great French playwrights Racine, Corneille, and Molière as well as a history of Christian attitudes toward polygamy, *After Polygamy Was Made a Sin* (1974).

In 1964, after Kim Philby had defected to the Soviet Union, Cairncross was again interrogated by MI5, and this time he confessed to espionage. British authorities decided not to prosecute him, perhaps in exchange for receiving information from Cairncross, and both sides agreed to remain silent on his past. Cairncross continued his literary studies and writing and also worked for the UN Food and Agriculture Organization in Rome. In 1990 and 1995 he was named as the "fifth man" in books by two former Soviet intelligence officers. In response, Cairncross moved back to England to prepare his memoirs, which were published as *The Enigma Spy: An Autobiography* two years after his death. Cairncross died on October 8, 1995. He insisted to the last that he had never betrayed secrets that damaged Britain, and he was not ashamed to admit that he had given the Soviet Union information it used to win its great victory at the Battle of Kursk.

CHAPTER FIVE

AMERICAN ROGUES AND DOUBLE AGENTS

I t can be argued that the United States, which assumed the mantle of leader of the West in the Cold War against the Soviet Union, had the most to gain and the most to lose from espionage. For the most part its intelligence agents functioned with the efficiency and discretion preferred in their profession. But the history of American spying during the Cold War is also punctuated by several sensational failures, including the politically charged case of Alger Hiss and Whittaker Chambers, the dismal saga of the Walker family, the bizarre fantasies of Jonathan Jay Pollard, and the frightening betrayals of Aldrich Ames and Robert Hanssen.

ALGER HISS

Alger Hiss was born on November 11, 1904, in Baltimore, Maryland. He graduated from Johns Hopkins University (A.B., 1926; Phi Beta Kappa) and Harvard Law School (1926–29) and was law clerk (1929–30) to Supreme Court Justice Oliver Wendell Holmes. In 1933 he entered government service in Pres. Franklin D. Roosevelt's administration and served successively in the Departments of Agriculture, Justice, and State. He attended the Yalta Conference (1945) as an adviser to Roosevelt and later served as temporary secretary-general of the United Nations (San Francisco

Alger Hiss testifying before the House Un-American Activities Committee hearings. Thomas D. McAvoy/Time& Life Pictures/ Getty Images

Conference). In 1946 he was elected president of the Carnegie Endowment for International Peace, a position he held until 1949.

In 1948 Whittaker Chambers, a self-professed former courier for a communist underground "apparatus" in Washington, D.C., accused Hiss of having been a member of the same "apparatus" before World War II. Hiss denied the charge, which was originally made before the House Committee on Un-American Activities. When Chambers repeated the charge publicly, away from the House committee chamber where his words were protected by congressional immunity, Hiss sued him for slander. On December 6, 1948, the House committee released sworn testimony by Chambers that Hiss had provided him (Chambers) with certain classified State Department papers for transmission to a Soviet agent. Hiss promptly denied the accusation "without qualification." In a federal grand-jury investigation of the case, both Chambers and Hiss testified; and Hiss was indicted on December 15 on two charges of perjury, specifically charging that Hiss lied both when he denied that he had given any documents to Chambers and when he testified that he did not talk to Chambers after January 1, 1937. Arraigned, Hiss pleaded not guilty. Hiss's first trial in 1949 ended in a hung jury. In the second trial, which ended early in 1950, he was found guilty. At both trials Chambers's sanity was a prominent issue.

The Hiss case, which came at a time of growing apprehension about the domestic influence of communism, seemed to lend substance to Sen. Joseph R. McCarthy's sensational charges of communist infiltration into the State Department. It also brought to national attention Richard M. Nixon, then a U.S. representative from California, who was prominent in the investigation that led to the indictment of Hiss.

After serving more than three years of a five-year prison sentence, Hiss was released in 1954, still asserting his innocence. During the following decades the issue of Hiss's guilt was kept open by outspoken defenders, principally from the American political left, who consistently maintained that he had been unjustly convicted. In 1992 Hiss asked Russian officials to check the newly opened archives of the former Soviet Union for information pertaining to the case. Later that year Gen. Dmitri A. Volkogonov, a historian and chairman of the Russian government's military intelligence archives, announced that a comprehensive search had revealed no evidence that Hiss had been involved in a Soviet spy ring. Many scholars, however, doubted that any search could divulge all the secrets of the complex Soviet intelligence operation—Volkogonov's search did not include Soviet military intelligence files—and therefore felt that the question of Hiss's innocence remained unresolved. In 1996 the release of secret Soviet cables that had been intercepted by U.S. intelligence during World War II provided strong evidence for Hiss's guilt. Hiss died on November 15, 1996, in New York City.

WHITTAKER CHAMBERS

Jay Vivian Chambers was born on April 1, 1901, in Philadelphia, Pennsylvania. He grew up on Long Island, New York, and attended Columbia University in New York City, where he studied alongside Meyer Schapiro, Herbert Solow, Louis Zukofsky, Clifton Fadiman, and Lionel Trilling and edited the university's literary journal the *Morningside* (later the *Columbia Review*). Because he disliked his given name, in the 1920s he assumed his mother's maiden name, Whittaker, as his given name. He joined

Whittaker Chambers testifying before the House Committee on Un-American Activities, 1948. Encyclopædia Britannica, Inc.

the Communist Party in the mid-1920s and wrote for the communist newspaper *The Daily Worker* (1927–29). He also wrote several articles for the Marxist publication *The New Masses*, of which he later became an editor (1931–32).

Chambers was asked to join the Soviet underground in 1932, serving first in New York. In the mid-1930s he moved to Baltimore after being assigned control of communists serving in and around Washington, D.C., in the U.S. federal government. As the Great Purge (purge trials, three widely publicized show trials and a series of closed, unpublicized trials held in the Soviet Union during the late 1930s, in which many prominent Old Bolsheviks were found guilty of treason and executed or imprisoned) mounted, Chambers deserted the Communist Party in April 1938. With the announcement of the German-Soviet Nonaggression Pact between Adolf Hitler and Joseph Stalin in August 1939, Chambers's friends, including the journalist Herbert Solow and Soviet defector Walter Krivitsky, urged and helped him to approach the administration of Pres. Franklin D. Roosevelt to warn about communist infiltration in the U.S. federal government. A meeting with U.S. Assistant Secretary of State Adolf A. Berle—a member of Roosevelt's group of advisers known as the Brain Trust—in September 1939 produced only Berle's meeting notes, which were filed away until they became evidence a decade later in the Hiss case.

In April 1939 Chambers joined *Time* magazine, where he held various writing and editorial positions before serving as special editor reporting to founder Henry R. Luce. Chambers helped articulate Luce's policy toward communism in his cover story on Stalin (February 1945), followed by a sensational "fairy tale" essay— *The Ghosts on the Roof* (March 1945; reprinted in January 1948)—about the Yalta Conference.

In August 1948 Chambers appeared under subpoena before the House Un-American Activities Committee (HUAC). When questioned, he identified Alger Hiss as one of seven government officials who had formed part of a communist spy ring in Washington, D.C., in the mid-1930s. Speaking without congressional protection on the political radio talk show *Meet the Press* later that month, Chambers responded positively to the question of whether or not Hiss had been a communist. In September 1948 Hiss filed a $75,000 slander suit against Chambers in Baltimore. During pretrial proceedings, lawyers for Hiss requested evidence from Chambers to support his allegations. Chambers subsequently submitted the "Baltimore Documents" (also known as the "Baltimore

Papers")—consisting of approximately 60 typewritten pages and several handwritten notes by Hiss and Harry Dexter White, the former chief international economist for the U.S. Department of the Treasury—which Chambers claimed to have stored inside a "life preserver" that he had prepared a decade earlier when he was defecting from the Soviet underground. Hiss in turn had the documents submitted to the U.S. Department of Justice in hope of securing an indictment against Chambers. Upon learning that Chambers still had evidence, HUAC member Richard M. Nixon subpoenaed all remaining evidence from Chambers at the beginning of December. Chambers had stored the remaining evidence (35-mm microfilm) in a hollowed-out pumpkin on his Maryland farm to avoid discovery. The press subsequently dubbed these artifacts the "Pumpkin Papers."

On December 15, 1948, a grand jury indicted Hiss on two counts of perjury—one for claiming that he had never given any documents to Chambers, and the other for claiming that he had not met with Chambers after January 1937. A first trial ended in a hung jury (1949), and a second ended with his conviction. Key evidence in the second trial—in addition to Chambers's testimony—were the Baltimore Documents, several of which contained Hiss's handwriting and others of which had been typed on a Woodstock typewriter belonging to Hiss. Upon his conviction, Hiss stated, "Until the day I die, I shall wonder how Whittaker Chambers got into my house to use my typewriter."

In 1952 Chambers published a best-selling autobiography, *Witness*, which was also serialized in *The Saturday Evening Post* and condensed in *Reader's Digest*. Aside from working briefly in the late 1950s as an editor for the *National Review* at the behest of founder William F. Buckley, Jr., Chambers hardly appeared in print again.

OLEG PENKOVSKY: SOVIET DOUBLE AGENT

In April 1961, a British businessman and secret agent, Greville M. Wynne, was approached by a senior Soviet military intelligence officer named Oleg Vladimirovich Penkovsky, who had become disillusioned with the Soviet system, particularly with the leadership of Nikita Khrushchev, and who offered his services to British intelligence. Between April 1961 and August 1962 Penkovsky passed more than 5,000 photographs of classified military, political, and economic documents to British and U.S. intelligence forces.

Penkovsky was born on April 23, 1919, in Vladikavkaz, Russia. He joined the Soviet Red Army in 1937 and served as an artillery officer in World War II, being severely wounded in 1944. He attended the prestigious Frunze Military Academy in 1945–48. In 1949 Penkovsky transferred from the regular army to the Soviet army intelligence directorate (GRU). After attending the Military Diplomatic Academy (1949–53), he became an intelligence officer, serving primarily in Moscow. By 1960 he had become a colonel in the GRU and deputy chief of the foreign section of the State Committee for the Coordination of Scientific Research (1960–62), in which post his task was to collect scientific and technical intelligence on the United States, Britain, and other Western countries. In that capacity he was probably the West's most valuable double agent during the Cold War. The information he provided on the Soviets' relatively weak capability in long-range missiles proved invaluable to the United States before and during the Cuban missile crisis of October 1962.

Penkovsky was in fact arrested by the Soviets on October 22, 1962, at the height of that crisis, after they realized that highly classified information was leaking to the West. Wynne, too, was arrested, while on a business trip to Budapest. The two were put on trial together in Moscow in May 1963. Wynne was found guilty of espionage and sentenced to eight years in prison, while Penkovsky was found guilty of treason and sentenced to death. According to an official Soviet announcement, Penkovsky was executed on May 16, 1963, though other reports have him committing suicide while in a Soviet camp. In 1965 his journal, *The Penkovskiy Papers*, was published in the United States, though the book's authenticity has been questioned. Wynne was exchanged in 1964 for a Soviet spy imprisoned in Britain; he resumed his business career and died of natural causes in 1990.

Chambers died on July 9, 1961, near Westminster, Maryland. Selections from his diaries and letters, edited by Fortune magazine managing editor Duncan Norton-Taylor, appeared as *Cold Friday* (1964). Pres. Ronald Reagan posthumously awarded Chambers the Presidential Medal of Freedom in 1984. In 1988 the Whittaker Chambers Farm was listed on the National Register of Historic Places.

JOHN WALKER

John Anthony Walker, Jr., was born on July 28, 1937, in Washington, D.C. His early life was troubled, with his family's stability threatened by his father's alcoholism. John dropped out of a Roman Catholic high school in West Scranton, Pennsylvania, during his junior year after attempting a burglary. Threatened with jail unless he joined the armed forces, he enlisted in the Navy and embarked on what appeared to be an exemplary career. From 1956 to 1975 he served as radioman on a succession of surface ships and nuclear submarines, rising to petty

The wooded area in Montgomery County, Maryland, where John Walker dropped off a shopping bag filled with classified U.S. documents for a KGB agent. The Washington Post/Getty Images

officer, chief petty officer, and warrant officer. During most of his naval career he worked with encryption codes and devices and had access to detailed information about the movements of both U.S. and Soviet fleets.

In 1967 Walker walked into the Soviet embassy in Washington, D.C., and offered to sell information. In return for substantial payments, which he felt he needed in order to repair a troubled marriage and personal finances, he regularly left photographed and photo-copied cryptographic keys, technical manuals, and other material in anonymous locations. He also periodically met his Soviet handlers in foreign locations such as Casablanca and Vienna. After retiring from the Navy in 1975, he opened a private detective business, but continued to obtain documents from Jerry Whitworth, a fellow radioman; his brother Arthur, a retired lieutenant commander who worked for a defense contractor; and his son, Michael, a petty officer assigned to a nuclear aircraft carrier.

Walker was arrested in May 1985 after his ex-wife and daughter informed the FBI of his spying. The rest of the spy ring was rounded up, and all were charged with passing navy secrets to Soviet agents. In return for a reduced sentence for Michael, John Walker agreed to plead guilty and to provide a detailed accounting of the material passed by him to the Soviets. He received a life sentence, his son 25 years, and his brother a $250,000 fine and life imprisonment. Whitworth, who refused to plead guilty to the charges, received the stiffest penalty of all, a $410,000 fine and 365 years in prison. Michael Walker was released from prison in 2000. The espionage activities of the Walker spy ring were described by some officials as among the gravest security breaches in the history of the U.S. Navy.

JONATHAN JAY POLLARD

Jonathan Jay Pollard was born on August 7, 1954, in Galveston, Texas. While he was young, his family moved to South Bend, Indiana, where his father was a professor of microbiology at the University of Notre Dame. He graduated from Stanford University in 1976. In 1977 he was rejected for a job with the CIA after an investigation uncovered his penchant for telling stories (some of which gave the impression that he was an agent of Israeli intelligence), and he began graduate studies at Tufts University in Medford, Massachusetts. In 1979, when he got a job at the Navy Operational Surveillance and Intelligence Center in Maryland, the CIA did not make its damaging report available to those investigating his fitness. Caught lying on the job in 1981, he was stripped of security clearance and told to seek psychiatric help, but his clearance was restored after he filed a grievance. In 1984 he was assigned to the navy's Anti-Terrorist Alert Center. With access to all government documents that could help with his job, he began to supply officials at the Israeli embassy who were connected to the Bureau of Scientific Relations with boxes and suitcases full of information from the Departments of State, Defense, and Justice as well as from the CIA and the National Security Agency. On October 25, 1985, he was seen carrying a large bundle from his office to his wife's car and was placed under surveillance. On November 21 he and his wife were arrested outside the Israeli embassy in Washington, where they had gone in hope of asylum.

Pollard's arrest caused acute embarrassment to Israel, whose officials were caught spying on a key ally. Israeli Prime Minister Shimon Peres apologized for Pollard's activities and dissolved the scientific intelligence agency that had recruited him. Pollard pled guilty to having conveyed classified information to a foreign state and cooperated with investigators. Nevertheless, in March 1987, he was given the maximum sentence of life in prison. His wife was sentenced to five years. At sentencing Pollard claimed to have been motivated by "sectarianism," though Israeli agents had agreed to pay him $30,000 each year for a period of ten years and had already paid him over $45,000. Secretary of Defense Caspar Weinberger wrote to the judge that Pollard had compromised sources of intelligence and had revealed the locations of ships.

Pollard entered the federal prison system in Marion, Illinois, and then transferred to Butner, North Carolina. His wife was released from a federal prison in Danbury, Connecticut, in 1989. In 1990 the couple divorced; Pollard remarried while in prison, and his first wife eventually moved to Israel. In 1996 the state of Israel granted Pollard citizenship. Numerous pro-Israel groups continued to call for Pollard's release from prison, as did Israeli officials and government leaders.

ALDRICH AMES

Aldrich Hazen Ames was born on June 26, 1941, in River Falls, Wisconsin. The son of an analyst for the CIA, he attended the University of Chicago for two years before becoming a CIA trainee in 1962; he also attended George Washington University (B.A., 1967). In 1969–72 Ames was posted to Ankara, Turkey, where he recruited U.S. spies from among Soviet nationals. He then lived in the United States until 1981, when he was posted to Mexico City. There he met his second wife, Maria del Rosario Casas Dupuy, a Colombian he recruited to work for the CIA. They married in 1985, while he was based again at CIA headquarters near Washington, D.C.; he was posted to Rome in 1986–89.

In 1985, aided by Rosario, who by then no longer worked for the CIA, Ames began selling American intelligence information to the KGB. At least 10 CIA agents within the Soviet Union were executed as a result of Ames's spying; ultimately, he revealed the name of every U.S. agent operating in the Soviet Union (after 1991, Russia). Before Aldrich and Maria Ames were arrested in 1994, they had received more than $2.7 million, the most money paid by the Soviet Union or Russia to any American for spying. Ames was convicted of espionage and sentenced to life in prison, and his wife received a five-year sentence for tax evasion and conspiracy to commit espionage. Ames was imprisoned in the high-security United States Penitentiary in Allenwood, Pennsylvania. His story was the topic of the 1998 film *Aldrich Ames: Traitor Within*.

ROBERT HANSSEN

Robert Philip Hanssen was born April 18, 1944, in Chicago, Illinois. The son of a police officer, he received a bachelor's degree from Knox College, Galesburg, Illinois, where he majored in chemistry but also studied Russian. At Northwestern University, Evanston, Illinois, he studied dentistry but then switched to business, earning a master's degree in accounting. In 1972 he joined the Chicago police force, where he became a member of a unit that investigated corrupt police officers. At this time he began to exhibit personal behaviour that marked him for the rest of his professional life—conservative dress and grooming, dour demeanour, awkward personal interaction, fervent anticommunist political beliefs, and adherence to a strict Roman Catholicism espoused by his wife, who was a member of the ultraconservative organization Opus Dei.

Robert Philip Hanssen. FBI/Getty Images

Hanssen joined the FBI in 1976. After two years as a criminal investigator in Gary, Indiana, he transferred to New York City, where he worked in the Bureau's Soviet counterintelligence unit. In 1979 he mailed an anonymous package to a Soviet trade office that was a front for the GRU, the Soviet military intelligence agency. The information in the package revealed the name of an FBI mole in the GRU, and for the next two years Hanssen sold similar information to the Soviets, earning about $20,000. After his wife discovered his espionage, he confessed his activities to an Opus Dei priest, promised to stop spying, and donated money to a Catholic charity.

In 1981 he was transferred to the FBI's Soviet Analytical Unit in Washington, D.C., where he had access to a treasure trove of information on the Bureau's counterintelligence work against the Soviet Union. Access continued from 1985 to 1987, when he supervised a technical surveillance squad in New York City, and from 1987, when he returned to Washington, serving as a supervisor in the Soviet Analytical Unit, as an aide in the Inspection Division, and as a program manager in the Soviet Section. In 1985 he began to spy for the KGB, the Soviet state intelligence agency. Using the alias "Ramon Garcia," he delivered documents and computer files on U.S. intelligence and counterintelligence activities at home and in the Soviet Union; this material revealed numerous double agents planted in the Soviet intelligence system, at least three of whom were arrested and executed. For his work Hanssen was paid at least $500,000 in cash plus jewelry. During this period his personal and professional behaviour deteriorated. He spent much time at work alone, frequently breached security protocols by mentioning classified information to people not authorized to know it, and spent large sums of money on gifts and foreign travel with a striptease dancer. Hanssen stopped selling secrets to the KGB in 1991, partly because of the collapse of the Soviet Union and possibly because he learned that the FBI was now hunting for a spy in its ranks.

In 1992 Hanssen became chief of the Bureau's National Security Threat List Unit in Washington, D.C. The following year he personally approached a GRU official with an offer to spy but was rebuffed; the Russians officially protested the incident, but an internal FBI inquiry led to no discipline against Hanssen. By 1995, however, he was deemed unsuitable for managerial responsibilities and was reassigned as a liaison between the FBI and the State Department's Office of Foreign Missions. He held this position for the rest of his career, working almost completely unsupervised. In 1999 he renewed contact with Russian foreign intelligence, delivering information on U.S. intelligence activities in Russia and counterintelligence activities in the United States. Meanwhile, the FBI continued its search for a mole, at first mistakenly investigating a CIA officer but finally settling on Hanssen (possibly using information provided by a Russian defector). In February 2001 Hanssen was arrested while placing a garbage bag containing secret information at a prearranged "dead drop" for pickup by his Russian handlers. In July he pleaded guilty to having spied for Moscow since 1979. As part of a plea deal, he avoided the death penalty by agreeing to participate in extensive debriefing with government agents. In 2002 Hanssen was given a sentence of life imprisonment without the possibility of parole. He was one of the Soviet Union's and Russia's most valuable double agents and the most damaging spy ever to penetrate the FBI.

CHAPTER SIX

INTELLIGENCE AGENCIES TODAY: THE U.S., SOVIET/RUSSIAN, AND BRITISH MODELS

Since the end of the Cold War, nonstate actors (e.g., terrorist organizations, militias, and drug cartels) have developed sophisticated intelligence and counterintelligence capabilities that rival those of some states. The Islamic terrorist organization al-Qaeda, which organized the September 11 attacks against the United States, had an intelligence infrastructure that maintained safe houses in the Middle East, Europe, and North America. Evidence uncovered after the U.S. and British military campaign in Afghanistan indicated that al-Qaeda had purchased sophisticated computer hardware that enabled it to send enciphered communications to terrorist cells and to track U.S. photographic reconnaissance satellites. Today, terrorists and drug traffickers from the jungles of Colombia to the streets of western Europe employ professional advisers and use criminals of various kinds to bribe or terrorize their opponents and protect their organizations. Accordingly, since the end of the Cold War the targets of intelligence activity are just as likely to be nonstate actors as states. Operations against such organizations require smaller and more-flexible intelligence services capable of combining technical intelligence (i.e., imagery and signals intelligence) and human intelligence; operations officers and analysts; and various military, intelligence, and security organizations.

For the organization of most intelligence services in this post–Cold War world, the intelligence systems of the three countries that were pillars of the Cold War—the United States, Russia, and the United Kingdom—are still used as general models. The American system has been adopted by many of the countries that came under U.S. influence after World War II; that of Russia was instituted in most Soviet-bloc countries; and that of the United Kingdom was used by most countries with parliamentary governments. The systems of these three countries are described below.

THE UNITED STATES

The decision to establish the CIA in 1947 reflected the United States's experience during World War II with the OSS and a postwar desire to create a central organization for defense. Since that time, the ideal of a single intelligence system has given way to the concept of an "intelligence community" comprising, among other agencies, the CIA, the Defense Intelligence Agency (DIA), separate army, navy, and air force intelligence staffs, the National Security Agency (NSA), and the FBI.

The CIA is under the jurisdiction of the National Security Council (NSC), chaired by the president. The National Security Act (1947), which has remained the basic charter for the organization of American intelligence, assigned the CIA five specific functions: (1) advising the NSC on intelligence matters related to national security, (2) recommending to the NSC measures for the efficient coordination of the intelligence activities of departments and agencies of government, (3) collecting and evaluating foreign intelligence and making certain that it is properly communicated within the government, (4) carrying out additional services for other intelligence agencies that the NSC determines can best be performed centrally, and (5) carrying out other functions and duties related to national security intelligence as the NSC may direct. The CIA also conducts secret political and economic intervention, psychological warfare, and paramilitary operations in other countries, functions that were treated as a Cold War necessity on the basis of a somewhat loose interpretation of the original charter.

Following the September 11 attacks in 2001 and the passage of the Homeland Security Act in the following year, CIA analysts were integrated into the intelligence sections of the new Department of Homeland Security. CIA officers also were assigned to work in FBI units, and FBI agents began to work at CIA headquarters. The post of director of national intelligence subsequently was established to coordinate the activities of the various intelligence agencies. The director also served as the president's chief adviser on intelligence.

The CIA comprises four major directorates responsible for intelligence, operations, administration, and science and technology. It is managed by a director and a deputy director, both appointed by the president and subject to Senate confirmation. The director of central intelligence (DCI) plays two distinct roles as both head of the CIA and a leading adviser to the president on intelligence matters relating to national security. The powers vested in the office of the DCI have increased over the years.

The principal role of the FBI is domestic counterintelligence. The FBI director serves under the attorney general in the Department of Justice. An assistant director of the FBI heads the National Security Division, whose budget, personnel, and organization are secret. The FBI and CIA cooperate in counterintelligence and counterterrorism and in efforts to combat international crime. The DIA and agencies of the armed services also perform counter-intelligence functions within their limited jurisdictions.

The NSA is the largest, most expensive, and perhaps least known of all U.S. intelligence organizations. Its basic function is signals intelligence—the making and breaking of codes and ciphers. Created by presidential directive in 1952, the NSA has remained, despite its enormous size and worldwide activities, the most secret of the acknowledged U.S. intelligence units; even the directive creating the agency remains secret. Headed by a high-ranking military officer, the NSA is under the jurisdiction of the secretary of defense but maintains a modest degree of autonomy. From its headquarters near Washington, D.C., the NSA conducts an immense variety of electronic espionage activities, many of which make use of sophisticated listening devices placed on planes and ships and in ground installations overseas. It is estimated that the NSA employs 20,000 people, but its activities also involve thousands of additional personnel from the armed services.

The DIA, established in 1961, is the major producer and manager of intelligence for the Department of Defense and is the principal adviser on military intelligence matters for the secretary of defense and the chairman of the Joint Chiefs of Staff. It supplies military intelligence for national reports and estimates, coordinates Department of Defense collection requirements (classified information requested by military commanders for planning and operational purposes), and manages the military attaché system. Although the agency is staffed by personnel from each of the armed services, more than half of all DIA employees are civilians.

Although the creation of the DIA sharply reduced the role of the separate armed forces intelligence services, each of them continues to perform significant tactical and technical intelligence and counterintelligence activities.

SERGEY OLEGOVICH TRETYAKOV: A POST–COLD WAR DEFECTOR

In 2000, Sergey Olegovich Tretyakov left his position as a colonel in the Russian Foreign Intelligence Service (SVR)—a successor agency of the Soviet KGB—to defect to the United States, where he gave the FBI and the CIA an estimated 5,000 secret cables and additional information about Russian intelligence operations and agents. Tretyakov was born on October 5, 1956, in Moscow. He studied at the Institute of Foreign Languages in Moscow and rose through the ranks of the KGB and, later, the SVR. By 1995 he was responsible for covert operations abroad while nominally serving the Russian government as a senior aide at the UN in New York City. He reportedly began supplying the U.S. with information in 1997, before leaving the SVR to live in hiding; American intelligence agencies allegedly rewarded his defection with a settlement of some $2 million. After the publication of Pete Earley's authorized biography *Comrade J.: The Untold Secrets of Russia's Master Spy in America After the End of the Cold War* (2007), Tretyakov lived openly under his real name. On June 13, 2010, he was found dead on the floor of his home in Osprey, Florida, having choked to death on the food he was eating for dinner.

Army intelligence is headed by the deputy chief of staff for intelligence. The Office of Naval Intelligence (ONI), headed by the director of naval intelligence, is responsible for foreign intelligence and cryptology. Air Force intelligence is headed by the director of intelligence, surveillance, and reconnaissance, who manages both technical and human intelligence programs.

The Department of Defense also controls the National Reconnaissance Office (NRO), one of several highly secret units that design, build, and operate satellites. Although it was created in the early 1960s, the NRO's existence was declassified only in 1992. Its size and importance have grown with advances in surveillance technology. Its programs are perhaps the most expensive—and useful—sources of intelligence available to the U.S. government.

RUSSIA

Until the Soviet Union's dissolution in the early 1990s, the KGB resembled a combination of the American CIA, FBI, and Secret Service (the agency charged with protecting the president and vice president and their families). This integration of foreign intelligence, counterintelligence, and internal security roles in a single agency was unusual, though the old Soviet system set the pattern for intelligence services in other communist countries. It is estimated that at the end of the Cold War the KGB had a staff of nearly 500,000 (excluding informers). About 20,000 KGB staff officers were employed in foreign intelligence, with the majority engaged in counterintelligence, surveillance of the public, technical intelligence, and border control. The KGB also controlled a large stable of informers, estimated by some to number 5 to 10 percent of the country's population.

During the late 1980s, as the Soviet government and economy were crumbling, the KGB survived better than most state institutions, suffering far fewer cuts in its personnel and budget. The agency was dismantled, however, after an attempted coup in August 1991 against Soviet leader Mikhail Gorbachev in which some KGB units participated. In early 1992 the internal security functions of the KGB were reconstituted first as the Ministry of Security and less than two years later as the Federal Counterintelligence Service (FSK), which was placed under the control of the president. In 1995 Russian Pres. Boris Yeltsin renamed the service the Federal Security Service (FSB) and granted it additional powers, enabling it to enter private homes and to conduct intelligence activities in Russia as well as abroad in cooperation with the Russian Foreign Intelligence Service (SVR).

Despite early promises to reform the Russian intelligence community, the FSB and the services that collect foreign intelligence and signals intelligence (the SVR and the Federal Agency for Government Communications and Information) remained largely unreformed and subject to little legislative or judicial scrutiny. Although some limits were placed on the FSB's domestic surveillance activities—for example, spying on religious institutions and charitable organizations was reduced—all the services continued to be controlled by KGB veterans schooled under the old regime. Moreover, few former KGB officers were removed following the agency's dissolution, and little effort was made to examine the KGB's operations or its use of informants.

In 1998 Yeltsin appointed as director of the FSB Vladimir Putin, a KGB veteran who would later succeed Yeltsin as federal president. Yeltsin also ordered the FSB to expand its operations against labour unions in Siberia and to crack down on right-wing dissidents. As president, Putin increased the FSB's powers to include countering foreign intelligence operations, fighting organized crime, and suppressing Chechen separatists.

The FSB, the largest security service in Europe, is extremely effective at counterintelligence. Human rights activists, however, have claimed that it has been slow to shed its KGB heritage. In addition, Russian intelligence in general suffers from various structural problems, including the problem that the information it produces is not always properly analyzed or acted upon.

THE UNITED KINGDOM

British intelligence was organized along modern lines as early as the reign of Queen Elizabeth I, and the long British experience has influenced the structure of most other systems. Unlike the intelligence agencies of the United States and the former Soviet Union, those of the United Kingdom historically have preserved a high degree of secrecy concerning their organization and operations. Even so, British intelligence has suffered from an unusually large number of native-born double agents.

The two principal British intelligence agencies are the Secret Intelligence Service (SIS; commonly known by its wartime designation, MI6) and the British Security Service (BSS; commonly called MI5). The labels derive from the fact that the Secret Intelligence Service was once "section six" of military intelligence and the Security Service "section five."

The British intelligence community is even more of a confederation of separate agencies than the U.S. intelligence community. Today, MI6 is a civilian organization largely resembling the U.S. CIA. It is charged with gathering information overseas and with other strategic services ranging from foreign espionage to covert political intervention. Its director, who is commonly referred to as "C," remains an almost anonymous figure. A high wall of secrecy likewise surrounds the rest of the organization; indeed, the British government barely acknowledges its existence, though an annual lump-sum appropriation request must be presented publicly to Parliament. The British services are much smaller than those of either the United States or Russia.

The expenditures of MI5 also are included in the annual budget submitted to Parliament. MI5 is roughly the

British equivalent of the U.S. FBI or the internal security (counterintelligence) section of the former Soviet KGB. However, it differs from the FBI in that it performs certain counterintelligence functions overseas. MI5's primary responsibility is to protect British secrets at home from foreign spies and to prevent domestic sabotage, subversion, and the theft of state secrets. The service is headed by a director general, who reports to the prime minister through the home secretary. The director general's traditional code name is "K"—a designation derived from the name of Sir Vernon Kell, its chief from 1909 to 1940. MI5 makes no direct arrests but instead works secretly with the more publicized "Special Branch" of Scotland Yard.

Another principal member of the British intelligence community is the Defence Intelligence Service, which resembles the American Defense Intelligence Agency. The service integrates into the Ministry of Defence intelligence specialists from the Royal Army, Navy, and Air Force. Another service is Communications Intelligence, which specializes in electronic surveillance and cryptology. Its operations are conducted from the Government Communications Headquarters (GCHQ) at Cheltenham.

MI6 is supervised by the Joint Intelligence Committee, a cabinet subcommittee under the permanent undersecretary of the foreign office. The Joint Intelligence Committee, which oversees all British intelligence agencies, controls intelligence policy and approves "national estimates" similar to those carried out by the U.S. National Intelligence Council. The British cabinet and parliamentary government affords a system of accountability lacking in the United States.

CHAPTER SEVEN

INTELLIGENCE AGENCIES TODAY: TWO GLOBAL HOT-SPOTS

By the 1970s every regional power and many relatively small states had developed intelligence services. In the multipolar world that arose following the Cold War, the services of several countries grew in importance, at least in the regions where they were located. Two of these regions are extremely important today: the Middle East and South Asia, where oil, militant Islam, and nationalism create a particularly dangerous mixture; and East Asia, where the economic powerhouse of China rises to preeminence while the lesser players Taiwan and South and North Korea present their own formidable challenges.

THE MIDDLE EAST AND SOUTH ASIA

Three nuclear-armed states—Israel, Pakistan, and India—and one state that many think aspires to join the nuclear club—Iran—present not just powerful militaries but also well-funded and highly capable intelligence systems. The activities of these countries' agencies have become more important as their respective governments have faced off against each other in serious regional rivalries.

ISRAEL

Since its creation in 1948, the State of Israel has met its obvious need for intelligence and counterintelligence with services that have gained a first-class reputation. One mark of their professionalism is that less is known about them than about other systems.

The Israeli intelligence establishment comprises several autonomous organizations. The Central Institute for Intelligence and Security, popularly known as Mossad, carries out foreign espionage and covert political and paramilitary operations, including the assassination of foreign figures. Its head reports directly to the prime minister.

Shin Bet, which takes its name from the Hebrew initials for General Security Services, conducts internal

Yuval Diskin (left), *head of Shin Bet (2005-11).* AFP/Getty Images

counterintelligence focused on potential sabotage, terrorist activities, and security matters of a strongly political nature. Shin Bet is divided into three wings responsible for Arab affairs, non-Arab affairs, and protective security—i.e., the protection of Israel's embassies, its defense

ISSER HAREL AND ADOLF EICHMANN

On May 11, 1960, Adolf Eichmann, the Nazi official responsible for carrying out the "final solution," the extermination of Jews in Europe, was arrested by Israeli secret service agents near Buenos Aires, Argentina. Nine days later the agents smuggled Eichmann out of the country and took him to Israel, where he was tried, sentenced to death, and executed in 1962.

The Israeli spymaster who directed the abduction was Isser Harel, born Isser Halper in 1912 in Vitebsk, Belorussia (now Belarus). In Palestine in 1942 Harel joined the clandestine Jewish organization Haganah, and two years later he became a member of Haganah's intelligence department. When Israel became independent in 1948, Harel became the first head of Shin Bet, Israel's internal intelligence agency. In 1952 he also became head of Mossad, the foreign intelligence agency. In 1960, he found and identified Eichmann where he was living in hiding in Buenos Aires, and organized his capture and transport to Israel.

Another campaign, against West German scientists who were helping Egypt develop weapons delivery systems at a time when the Israeli government was developing closer ties to West Germany, caused Prime Minister David Ben-Gurion to require his resignation in 1963. Harel's account of the Eichmann capture, *The House on Garibaldi Street* (1975), made him famous. He died on February 18, 2003, at Petah Tiqwa, Israel.

infrastructure, and El Al, the national airline. In the 1990s Shin Bet came under international scrutiny for its use of torture against some Palestinian detainees and for its role in the assassinations of alleged Palestinian militants. It also was criticized for its failure to prevent the assassination of Prime Minister Yitzhak Rabin in November 1995. In the aftermath of the ensuing scandal, the head of Shin Bet was forced to resign.

The Intelligence Corps of the Defense Forces, commonly referred to as Military Intelligence (or Aman), constitutes a third major Israeli intelligence organization. Some observers view it as a rival to Mossad, and conflicts between the two agencies have been reported. Its chief is the military intelligence adviser to the minister of defense.

The Lekem Bureau of Scientific Relations was a small, clandestine intelligence organization that recruited spies in Western countries until it was disbanded in 1986 following the arrest of Jonathan Jay Pollard, a U.S. naval intelligence analyst who sold highly classified U.S. intelligence documents to Israel. According to some sources, the duties of the bureau have been assumed by an office in the Ministry of Foreign Affairs.

IRAN

Prior to the Islamic revolution of 1978–79 in Iran, SAVAK (Organization of National Security and Information), the Iranian secret police and intelligence service, protected the regime of the shah by arresting, torturing, and executing many dissidents. After the shah's government fell, SAVAK and other intelligence services were eliminated and new services were created, though many low- and mid-level intelligence personnel were retained or rehired by the new services. The most important of the postrevolutionary intelligence services is the Ministry

Nematollah Nasiri, director of SAVAK (1965-78). AFP/Getty Images

of Intelligence and Security (MOIS), which is responsible for both intelligence and counterintelligence. It also has conducted covert actions outside Iran in support of Islamic regimes elsewhere; for example, it was said to have provided military support to Muslim fighters in Kosovo and in Bosnia and Herzegovina in the 1990s. Since then it has been accused of providing assistance to the Lebanese Shī'ite group Hezbollah, the Palestinian Islamic group Hamas, and al-Qaeda in Iraq, among others.

Shortly after the Islamic revolution, the new regime formed an impromptu militia known as the Revolutionary Guards (Persian: Pāsdārān-e Enqelāb), or simply as the Pāsdārān, to forestall any foreign-backed coup—such as the one the CIA had undertaken to topple the nationalist prime minister Mohammad Mosaddeq in 1953—and to act as a foil to the powerful Iranian military. The Pāsdārān also aided the country's new rulers in running the country and enforcing the government's Islamic code of morality. Only after Iraq invaded Iran in 1980 was the organization pressed into a broader role as a conventional military force; at the same time, the Pāsdārān—which answered to its own independent ministry—sought to broaden its scope by developing departments for intelligence gathering (both at home and abroad) and clandestine activities. The names and functions of these departments are not well-known. One such group, however, is known as the Qods (Jerusalem) Force. Like the MOIS, it is responsible for conducting clandestine operations and for training and organizing foreign paramilitary groups in other parts of the Islamic world.

PAKISTAN

The intelligence community of Pakistan is one of the most sophisticated in the world. The ISI (Inter-Service

Intelligence), which is responsible to the General Staff of the Ministry of Defense, has undertaken major foreign intelligence and covert operations, such as the funding and training of Afghan partisans during their guerrilla war against the Soviet Union in the 1980s and the arming and training of the Taliban movement before the terrorist bombings against the United States in September 2001. In addition, the ISI allegedly provides close support to separatists in the disputed territory of Kashmir, and it has been accused by U.S. officials of retaining links to Taliban-affiliated groups that have found sanctuary in Pakistan. In addition to the ISI, separate tactical intelligence services are maintained by the three branches of the Pakistani military. The Intelligence Bureau carries out domestic surveillance against the general population.

INDIA

India, which has fought several wars with Pakistan since the 1940s, also has a sophisticated intelligence community; unlike that of Pakistan, it is accountable to the civilian government. The Joint Intelligence Committee, which is supervised by the Cabinet Secretariat, analyzes information collected by civilian and military agencies. Military intelligence is the province of the Directorates of Military Intelligence, Naval Intelligence, and Air Intelligence, and the Joint Cipher Bureau provides interservice cryptology and signals intelligence. India's most important intelligence agency is a civilian service, the Research and Analysis Wing (RAW). The RAW's operations are for the most part confined to the Indian subcontinent, including Bangladesh, Sri Lanka, and Pakistan. The RAW also has directed efforts in the United States aimed at influencing that government's foreign policy.

Domestic security and counterintelligence are the responsibility of agencies controlled by the Union Ministry of Home Affairs, which has overall control of the country's police and domestic counterintelligence. A number of paramilitary internal security organizations have been created for operations in Kashmir, the Indian-Tibetan border, and other regions where there has been unrest and insurgency. The record of these organizations is mixed; though they have strong professional leadership, they have been blamed for atrocities against civilians and suspected guerrillas. Internal security is the responsibility of the Intelligence Bureau (IB), which performs a role similar to that of the American FBI. Following the Mumbai terrorist attacks of 2008, which were carried out by members of a Pakistani terrorist group, a new National Investigation Agency (NIA) was set up under the Ministry of Home Affairs specifically to investigate and prevent terrorist attacks that affect relations with foreign countries.

EAST ASIA

The great military power of this region, nuclear-armed China, has intelligence services that have become especially prominent—particularly in the area of industrial espionage and cyberespionage. At the same time, Taiwan continues to assert itself as an alternative Chinese model, and the deadly Cold War rivals of South and North Korea continue to assess and probe each other's strengths and weaknesses.

CHINA

Foreign intelligence and counterintelligence in China is the province of the MSS (Ministry of State Security).

The organization of the MSS is similar to that of the former Soviet KGB, with bureaus responsible for foreign intelligence, counterintelligence, and the collection of scientific and technical intelligence. Chinese intelligence operations are conducted by officers under diplomatic cover as well as under nonofficial cover as businessmen and scholars. Its operations have been fairly successful, especially in the United States. In 2000, for example, a U.S. congressional committee concluded that Chinese intelligence "stole classified information on every currently deployed U.S. intercontinental ballistic missile (ICBM) and submarine-launched ballistic missile (SLBM)."

The Military Intelligence Department of the General Staff Department of the People's Liberation Army (PLA) is China's second largest intelligence organization. It collects information through military attachés and intelligence officers under academic and business cover. The PLA, the navy, and the air force also collect human intelligence and signals intelligence. Although little is known about Chinese signals intelligence, it is believed to be controlled by the Sixth Bureau of the air force staff. It is believed that cyberespionage, cyberdefense, and cyberattack are conducted by several organizations, such as the General Staff Department Third and Fourth Departments, at least six Technical Reconnaissance Bureaus, and a number of PLA Information Warfare Militia Units.

The Chinese communist leadership always has been concerned with dissent, whether political, social, or religious. Both the People's Armed Police and the MSS closely watch suspected dissidents. During the 1990s and into the 21st century, members of the Chinese spiritual movement Falun Gong frequently were harassed and arrested by the authorities.

The Chinese Communist Party collects foreign intelligence independently of the MSS and the armed forces. The International Liaison Department of the General Political Department of the Communist Party Central Committee carries out operations in the United States and Taiwan.

TAIWAN

As part of its democratization process at the end of the 20th century, the government of Taiwan took major steps to reform its intelligence services. The once-covert National Security Bureau, developed in China in 1955, had a long history of clandestine arrests and executions. In 1994 it became a formal legal institution, and the names of its senior officials appeared in the press for the first time. The agency, which is under the jurisdiction of the National Security Council, is responsible for all aspects of the country's intelligence, including foreign and counterintelligence and intelligence related to mainland China.

SOUTH KOREA

As in Taiwan, South Korea's intelligence community, originally established in the 1960s with U.S. guidance, underwent major changes beginning in the 1990s. The Korean Central Intelligence Agency and its successor, the Agency for National Security Planning, were deeply involved in domestic politics and human rights abuses, especially during the period of martial law in the 1980s. In 1994 legislative oversight of the agency was strengthened, and in the following year it moved to a new headquarters complex under new leadership. The agency, renamed the National Intelligence

Service in 1999, collects and coordinates national security intelligence. The Defense Security Command of the Ministry of National Defense and the National Intelligence Service are responsible for the collection of national security intelligence, particularly with regard to the threat from North Korea. The Defense Security Command also handles counterintelligence within the military.

NORTH KOREA

Far less is known about the intelligence community in North Korea, where intelligence and counterintelligence operations are apparently controlled by the Cabinet General Intelligence Bureau, a component of the Central Committee of the ruling Korean Workers' (Communist) Party. The party also controls a semisecret organization, the General Association of Korean Residents in Japan (Chosen Soren), that collects information and money from expatriate citizens. The Chosen Soren, whose name derives from the formal name of Korea when it was controlled by Japan, has been pivotal in helping North Korea to acquire advanced technology. Because Japan does not maintain formal diplomatic relations with North Korea, the Chosen Soren serves as North Korea's de facto embassy and intelligence service in Japan. Much of the country's counterintelligence is the responsibility of the State Safety and Security Agency, which functions as a secret police force and administers camps for political prisoners. The Social Safety Ministry, the country's police force, is among North Korea's most powerful agencies, maintaining prisons, conducting investigations of potential opponents of the regime, and protecting leading officials.

North Korea has a large military intelligence system. The Reconnaissance Bureau of the General Staff Department of the Ministry of People's Armed Forces, which is believed to control between 60,000 and 100,000 troops, undertook violent covert action during the Cold War, including the assassination of senior South Korean officials and the sabotage of a South Korean airliner. Beginning in the early 1990s, North Korea made several efforts to land agents in South Korea from fishing trawlers and miniature submarines. It also bored tunnels under the demilitarized zone between North and South Korea to infiltrate agents into the South.

In January 2013, North Korea announced that the United States was the "sworn enemy of the Korean people" and that it intended to target America in its nuclear programs. Then in March 2013, in a move that further isolated the "Hermit Kingdom," North Korea declared the 1953 Korean War armistice nullified in response to the financial sanctions imposed on it in UN Resolution 2094.

During the great ideological conflicts of World War II and the Cold War, the exploits of spies and counterspies became a staple of the entertainment and publishing industries. In books, movies, and television, intelligence agents were portrayed in roles that were sometimes comic but most often dramatic and at times deadly serious. All these accounts tended to glamorize an occupation that in reality was painfully tedious and sometimes (in the opinion of some) distasteful and immoral. Yet in spite of its dubious moral standing it was a job that had to be done—and, given the incomparably high stakes for everybody concerned, it had to be done in secret.

During the Cold War some national intelligence systems, especially those in the major countries, grew beyond a size that was necessary for the world that came after. In addition, they were accustomed to working with a certain freedom of action and absence of oversight that became obsolete with the end of the Cold War. Even today, in both democracies and authoritarian societies, intelligence organizations are in a position to demand that their operations and the information they collect be kept secret, not only from the public but also from most government officials. This need for secrecy, though legitimate in theory, obviously makes adequate oversight difficult to achieve in practice. The problem of secrecy is especially acute in countries where the intelligence services historically have been used as vehicles of political conspiracy and intrigue. In part because of rapidly advancing technology, intelligence systems are likely to grow in power and autonomy in the 21st century. In order to avoid becoming virtual prisoners of their need for security, citizens of all countries, through their legislative and executive bodies, must be cognizant of the need for effective policy controls over the services that collect information at home and beyond their borders.

GLOSSARY

cipher A combination of symbolic letters.

clandestine Marked by, held in, or conducted with secrecy.

Cold War The ideological conflict between the United States and the Union of Soviet Socialist Republics during the second half of the 20th century.

communism A doctrine based on revolutionary Marxian socialism and Marxism-Leninism that was the official ideology of the Union of Soviet Socialist Republics.

counterintelligence Organized activity of an intelligence service designed to block an enemy's sources of information, to deceive the enemy, to prevent sabotage, and to gather political and military information.

covert Not openly shown, engaged in, or avowed.

cryptography The enciphering and deciphering of messages in secret code or cipher or the computerized encoding and decoding of information.

dissident Someone who breaks from an established religious or political system, organization, or belief.

double agent A spy pretending to serve one government while actually serving another.

drone An unmanned aircraft used to secretly gather information or conduct military strikes.

espionage The practice of spying or using spies to obtain information about the plans and activities, usually of a foreign government.

fascism A political philosophy, movement, or regime (as that of the Fascisti) that exalts nation and often race above the individual and that stands for a centralized autocratic government headed by a dictatorial leader, severe economic and social regimentation, and forcible suppression of opposition.

guerrilla A person who engages in irregular warfare especially as a member of an independent unit carrying out harassment and sabotage.

hacking: Illegally gaining access to and sometimes tampering with information in a computer system.

intelligence Information concerning an enemy or possible enemy or an area.

left-wing The liberal division of a group (as a political party)

Leninism Principles expounded by Vladimir Lenin to guide the transition of society from capitalism to communism.

Marxism The political, economic, and social principles and policies advocated by Karl Marx; a theory and practice of socialism including the labor theory of value, dialectical materialism, the class struggle, and dictatorship of the proletariat until the establishment of a classless society.

ministry The body of ministers governing a nation or state from which a smaller cabinet is sometimes selected.

propaganda The spreading of ideas, information, or rumor for the purpose of helping or injuring an institution, a cause, or a person.

reconnaissance A preliminary survey to gain information, such as an exploratory military survey of enemy territory.

right-wing The conservative division of a group or party.

slander The utterance of false charges or misrepresentations which defame and damage another's reputation.

surveillance Close watch kept over someone or something.

treason The offense of attempting by overt acts to overthrow the government of the state.

BIBLIOGRAPHY

General works on intelligence include Mark M. Lowenthal, *Intelligence: From Secrets to Policy* (2000); Walter Laqueur, *A World of Secrets: The Uses and Limits of Intelligence* (1985, reissued 1993); and Abram N. Shulsky and Gary J. Schmitt, *Silent Warfare: Understanding the World of Intelligence*, 3rd ed., rev. (2002). A helpful analysis of intelligence in the post-Cold War world is Robert M. Clark, *Intelligence Analysis: A Target-Centric Approach* (2003).

HISTORICAL AND COMPARATIVE WORKS

Works on signals intelligence are David Kahn, *The Codebreakers: The Story of Secret Writing*, rev. ed. (1996); Stephen Budiansky, *Battle of Wits* (2002), a graceful history of the role of signals intelligence in the Allied victory in World War II; and Ronald Lewin, *The American Magic: Codes, Ciphers, and the Defeat of Japan* (also published as *The Other Ultra*, 1982), and *Ultra Goes to War: The First Account of World War II's Greatest Secret Based on Official Documents* (1978, reissued 2001). General discussions of the World War II era include William Casey, *The Secret War Against Hitler* (1988); and David Kahn, *Hitler's Spies: German Military Intelligence in World War II* (2000).

Intelligence surveillance from space during the Cold War years is discussed in William E. Burrows, *Deep Black: Space Espionage and National Security* (1986).

Two comparative analyses are Roy Godson (ed.), *Comparing Foreign Intelligence: The U.S., the USSR, the U.K. & the Third World* (1988); and Nigel West, *Games of Intelligence: The Classified Conflict of International Espionage* (1989), addressing intelligence operations in the United States, France, the former Soviet Union, Israel, and the United Kingdom.

NATIONAL INTELLIGENCE SYSTEMS

The CIA's role is discussed in Jeffrey T. Richelson, *The U.S. Intelligence Community*, 5th ed. (2008). A critical history of the CIA is provided in Tim Weiner, *Legacy of Ashes: The History of the CIA* (2007). An excellent account of the Office of Strategic Services is Joseph E. Persico, *Roosevelt's Secret War: FDR and World War II Espionage* (2001). Christopher Andrew, *For the President's Eyes Only: Secret Intelligence and the American Presidency from Washington to Bush* (1995), provides a good overview of U.S. intelligence during that period. Robert M. Gates, *From the Shadows: The Ultimate Insider's Story of Five Presidents and How They Won the Cold War* (1993, reissued 1996), is an insider's account by a former CIA director. The covert operations of the CIA have been discussed in the works of many former operations officers, including Antonio Mendez, *The Master of Disguise: My Secret Life in the CIA* (1999); William J. Daugherty, *In the Shadow of the Ayatollah* (2001); and David Atlee Phillips, *The Night Watch* (1977).

The history of British intelligence is detailed in Christopher Andrew, *Secret Service: The Making of the British Intelligence Community* (1986); and F.H. Hinsley et al., *British Intelligence in the Second World War*, 5 vol.

(1979–90), an official account, based on the authors' access to secret archives, available also in a 1-vol. abridged version with the same title (1993). Aspects of the early Cold War years are covered in Stephen Dorril, *MI-6: Inside the Covert World of Her Majesty's Secret Intelligence Service* (2000); and Nigel West, *Molehunt: The Full Story of the Soviet Spy in MI5* (1987).

Descriptions and histories of the KGB include Yevgeniya Albats, *The State Within a State: The KGB and Its Hold on Russia—Past, Present and Future* (1994); Oleg Kalugin, *The First Directorate* (1994), the personal account of a Soviet intelligence officer; and Christopher Andrew and Oleg Gordievsky, *KGB: The Inside Story of Its Foreign Operations from Lenin to Gorbachev* (1990). An excellent account of Soviet intelligence in the 1930s is Gary Kern, *A Death in Washington: Walter G. Krivitsky and the Stalin Terror* (2003). An account of the Soviet effort to steal American nuclear secrets is Alexander Feklisov, *The Man Behind the Rosenbergs* (2001). An excellent history of KGB operations in the United States is Allen Weinstein and Alexander Vasiliev, *The Haunted Wood* (2000). The struggle between the KGB and the CIA in the last decades of the 20th century is the subject of Milt Bearden and James Risen, *The Main Enemy: The Inside Story of the CIA's Final Showdown with the KGB* (2003).

Accounts of Israeli intelligence include Gordon Thomas, *Gideon's Spies: The Secret History of the Mossad* (1999); Samuel Katz, *Soldier Spies* (1994); and Ian Black, *Israel's Secret Wars* (1991).

INDEX